Where's My Mom and Dad?

Where's My Mom and Dad?

Ivanhoe Chaput

Table of Contents

INTRODUCTION

My mom's passing in 2010 inspired this book. Anyone that's lost a loved one must at some time wonder where that loved one really went after leaving here. Pastors, priests or maybe the funeral director eulogizes our deceased loved one with words that come from the Bible or some other religiously inspired writings. But that doesn't take away the feeling of loss. Friends will share in your loss, but not to the degree that a son, a daughter, a father or a mother will. They will forget and move on with their lives, but we, the very ones that are connected by the code within the DNA molecule, carry the memory of their existence and their connection with us each and every day.

Some of us will actually perceive that signs are coming from them, from the other side. Most of us sense a presence that they are still with us in some form. But three in four people believe that they are simply gone, that they are nowhere. Skeptics will say that signs from the other side are tricks of the mind stemming from a strong desire to believe that their loved one is not "nowhere." This might be the case in some instances. In contrast to this, there are cases that are beyond materialistic explanation.

My search for where my mom and dad are, is not a turnstile into religious ideologies, an engagement into a faith-based belief or to justify my belief that they are "somewhere." It's not some mystic epiphany. It was a pragmatic search based on evidence that I could not discard. This story starts as a child with a strong belief in God, to vacillating between agnostic and atheist for some thirty-five years, to a conviction that there is an afterlife.

Although I had looked into near-death experiences out of curiosity prior to my parents' deaths, it was my mom's passing that motivated me to search for an answer to my haunting question, "Where's my mom and dad?" This moved me to immerse myself into the phenomenon of veridical near-death experiences. I'm not an expert, but the evidence conclusively solved my question. This work comprises philosophical ideas, factual research, and physics that support solid evidence of the concept of consciousness without the physical body.

As a society and a global family, we are collectively ignorant as to the final reality of death. We are steeped in beliefs stemming from ancient ideas and, recently, we are reeling from the constraints of the scientific method. Beliefs hang on for generations like a bad stain on a carpet. It cannot be lifted without much effort. If someone walks off the edge of a building they will fall. This provided evidence that supported the idea that the world was flat; if one went out far enough, they would fall off the edge. The idea that the world was round didn't have much support amongst the intelligentsia of the time when the world was flat.

As Columbus climbed higher on a mountain, he observed that he could see ship's sails farther out in the ocean. The idea that the world was spherical, like the moon, gave birth to a new paradigm.

We tend to hang onto old beliefs. Too often new and constructive ideas about our existence are impeded by outdated entrenched beliefs. It's the brave explorers that are willing to stake their reputations by presenting new and sometimes very radical ideas that are the result of empirical evidence. Too often evidence is not enough to sway the minds of those whose feet are firmly planted in their traditions. Beliefs can be the anchors that hold back the very substance of progress.

Pathmakers face the challenge of influencing traditions taught by scholars who were taught by previous scholars. Respect for the intelligentsia fed the belief that these scholars knew what was going on in the halls of knowledge, the universities and traditional religious institutions. Changes in beliefs occur so slowly that the Flat Earth Society still exists today and conspiracy theorists still believe that our trips to the moon were done on a sound stage. .

Hence, the resistance of old beliefs pushes against evidence of new discoveries. The atheists will hang onto their beliefs, and the traditionally religious will hang onto theirs, despite evidence to the contrary. We are experiencing a revelation of knowledge about the afterlife with a deluge of people writing their stories of what happened to them when they were dead. My purpose is not to take sides as to who is right and who is wrong, but to further advance the evidence about our inevitable journey. What we believe entraps us within the confines of those beliefs. Unless we open our minds to these new possibilities based on certain incontrovertible evidence, we will remain encapsulated in beliefs that may be in opposition to the obvious.

Although my mom's passing inspired this work, it was the sheer volume of evidence that compelled me to write about the dead—that we simply don't die. The evidence clearly supported the fact that we can have total faculty of consciousness outside our bodies. The evidence supports that heaven is not a place, but an environment of the mind in which love and God breathes.

PROLOGUE

For Ivanhoe Chaput, grief was like a box that threw everything into unknown darkness. The loss of Mom and Dad dropped a shadow on him like a looming thundercloud that he couldn't shed. His thoughts drifted throughout the day as the memories of Mom and Dad overarched whatever he was doing. "They're gone. I'll never see them again."

Then signs began to appear that reminded him of them. "Could this be for real? Are they really still with me and I just can't see them?"

Follow a six-year journey that culminates in factual support that we are not our brains. We don't die. Discover evidence that supports an afterlife where souls, our departed loved ones, comprise consciousness. Find out why our earthly existence is replete with pain, violence, death and war. Identify the realms where hell is distinguished from ascension into a pure heaven of love.

Thousands of people are coming forward with their experiences of having been to the other side and come back to tell their stories. Find out why the accounts at first appear to make no sense until a big picture begins to shed some correlation between these diverse experiences. There is a God. The discovery that He does not judge, that love is what permeates the universe, brought light into Ivanhoe's shadow of grief.

CHAPTER 1

MY MOM AND DAD

Who were my mom and dad? What was special about them? Actually, they were just normal people.

My mom was born Colombe Mary Meilleur on June 22, 1922 and died on August 16, 2010. My dad, Joseph Alexis Edouard Chaput, was born June 13, 1915 and died on February 4, 1994.

My mom's name, Colombe, means "dove" in French. There's a French song by a singer named Johnny Hess written in 1943 that goes, "Colombe, Colombe, petit oiseau d'amour," which means, "Dove, dove, little bird of love." Mom fit this to a T.

My mom always called my dad "Eddie." While many people called him Eddie after we moved to America, most renamed him "Frenchie" because of his heavy French accent. Mom never had an accent, in French or English. She was perfectly bilingual.

Mom and Dad were both Gemini. Although I'm not into astrology, I decided to look up what Geminis are all about. To my delight, I found that the description perfectly matches them both!

Geminis are always probing into things in search for information. Geminis also love to have fun and develop relationships. Twins represent them, since Geminis are a mix of yin and yang. They can easily see both sides of an issue, which is a wonderfully practical quality. They are quick thinking, quick witted and fast on their feet. They are curious, clever and are a hit at parties. They are the clearest of thinkers and put out logical, well-thought-out ideas.

One Gemini trait that stood out for me was that their lightness of spirit and youthful exuberance help them to appear forever young. The great strength of the Gemini-born is in their ability to communicate effectively. Adventures of the mind are what the Twins are all about. They also love to share themselves with their friends, and they make for charming companions.

If I had kept a voice recorder on during any one of their normal evenings at home in their last years, you would not be able to guess that they were past thirty. They were always engaged in conversation with seldom a pause, unless my dad was reading his newspaper, which he loved to do. He kept up with current affairs on TV and loved his home on the lake. My mom kept up with relentless servitude, making sure that my dad was well fed and kept the fridge well stocked with beer. My dad loved his beer.

Although my dad was the king of his castle, we knew that it was my mom that ran the business of keeping everything in order. I have to say that even though they were similar in many ways, and it's often that opposites attract, they were nonetheless a perfect match, even though they did engage in disagreements when Dad was feeling his barley, that stuff beer is made from.

Dad grew up in a little rural Canadian community called Lanoraie. His dad was a farmer. Dad had five brothers and one sister. When we vacationed in Canada, all the aunts and uncles would get together and recount stories of living on the farm as youngsters. They told of one time when they placed a full bucket of water over the door of one of their neighbors, knocked on the door and ran. When the neighbor opened the door, the bucket tipped and the poor neighbor got a soaking. What do kids do with no TV or cell phones?

Another story was about the time they stuck a needle between the glass and the caulking of one neighbor's window, tied a thread to the needle that led to some bushes and hid in them. They rubbed the thread with violin resin until it began to screech. With the top of the needle against the window, the glass acted like a speaker and was extremely loud. When the neighbor heard this, he went to the window to see what was happening. Since the needle and thread were so small, and the thread ran out to the bushes where the pranksters were hiding, the neighbor saw nothing and returned to what he was doing. Then, again, *screeeech* went the needle against the window, where the neighbor again went to investigate. At the time, there were no flashlights and no electricity where they lived. Candles and kerosene lamps provided all the lighting and didn't put out much. After several times of coming out, the neighbor finally caught on that it was another prank being pulled by the little Chaput kids, for which they were famous. This one I thought was particularly creative.

In my company, I have a saying that I use when we need to improvise on some task that's tricky or that we need to accomplish with only the materials we have. I call it, "Grandpa's tractor." My grandfather couldn't afford to buy a tractor, but he needed one after their horse, Little Lou, died. So the Chaput brothers went all over town collecting parts of vehicles and built what can only be described as the platypus of tractors. It consisted of an old car body that had its top and most of its sides chopped off, a rear transaxle from a scrapped truck, front wheels off another car, large rear wheels off an old road grater and other miscellaneous parts. I've included a photo of Grandpa's tractor for you to get a look at my dad's and his brother's creative powers. The little boy sitting in the seat is my brother, who's now seventy-four.

My dad grew up to be a tool and die maker and loved making things both at his work and at home. In his retired years he made birdhouses in his garage. He would make them and give them to his neighbors around the lake community where he retired. Some of these were multi-story apartment-looking complexes; some were churches with steeples and colored windows; some looked like Swiss cuckoo clocks while some looked like, well, birdhouses. Dad was generous with his time and people around the lake appreciated what he did for them.

Mom was born in Ontario, Canada. Her family moved to Spokane, Washington when she was fourteen, driving their 1935 Ford cross-country, then moved to Montreal somewhere around sixteen. Most people that learn another language at sixteen years old will have a bit of an accent. Mom picked it up and mastered the French language with no accent. She was eighteen when she got a job in a shoe factory where she met my Uncle Luke, one of my dad's brothers. As the story goes, she and Uncle Luke dated for a short while and my dad liked her very much. I don't know how it happened, but she must have dumped my Uncle Luke when she took a liking for my dad. They got together, fell in love and got married in 1940. My mom was eighteen and my dad was twenty-five. That's about all I know of their early romance, except for hundreds of old pictures of what appears to be a grand old time.

Mom would refer to my dad as "a handsome devil." He looked like a movie star named Don Ameche. My dad always called her, "Beautiful Mama." Mom was beautiful in many more ways than just her looks!

I once asked my dad what he liked the most about Mom. I was sure he would say something like her cooking, or how hard she worked to keep the house clean and together. His answer was, "The way she walks from behind."

My brother was born in 1942 and I was born in 1947. In 1952 we moved from Montreal to Ohio. We bought a tiny little house in Geauga Lake, Ohio and added onto it. Mom and Dad designed and expanded onto the kitchen, making it twice as large overall, and the living room twice as big. They built a really nice fireplace and a single-car garage that was attached to the kitchen portion of the house. My mom and dad did all the work themselves. I don't know where my dad got the knowledge to build onto this house, but he always did whatever he set his mind to do. He was very talented, and my mom always said, "He could make anything."

To make a long introduction short, I'll jump ahead to their house on Lake Cavalier in Mississippi some twelve years later. There's more to say in Chapter 3 about our interesting Arizona experience on the journey between Ohio and Mississippi.

While living in the house on the lake, my mom always planted a garden on their acre of land. It wasn't because they needed to save money so they didn't have to spend so much on groceries, but mainly for the love of gardening. Mom planted many flowers and plants of all sorts to adorn their humble house. She even planted a banana tree that produced a bunch of small bananas. I don't know why they were so small.

Mom was the workhorse in the family. She was a strong redheaded gal, and you never wanted to get into the path of her displeasure. On the other hand, she would sacrifice her life for anyone in the family, and even for a stranger. To get to know my mom and dad a bit, I've picked out an event that characterizes her and a couple that characterize my dad.

This event sums up my mom, who she really was.

I was about four and a half years old when we were living in St. Genevieve, Canada. Mom and Dad were renting a little house right on the banks of the Prairies River. Our house was right next to a bridge crossing the river. After sixty-four and a half years, to my surprise, I found it still standing in Google Maps and added it in the picture section.

I was playing at the river's bank with two twins. We must have been the same age, four and a half years old. We were having fun throwing rocks into the fast moving river. It was early spring and the current was strong from all the melting ice and snow. My mom was hanging wet clothes on the clothesline that ran from the porch to a nearby tree. It was very cold because I remember little chunks of ice floating in the water. One of the twins picked up a rock to throw it into the river when he slipped and slid off its banks right into the turbulent water. The current sucked him out away from the shore and his head went bobbing up and down, in and out of the top of the waves caused by rocks on the river's bottom.

When Mom saw what had happened, without an ounce of hesitation she dropped her clothespins and ran full speed to the river's bank. She didn't stop there. I remember this like it was yesterday. She didn't jump into the water; she didn't wade into the water; she dove headfirst into the icy fast-flowing water to swim after the twin to save his life. The internal feeling I had, seeing not only the boy fall into the turbulent water, but then seeing my mom disappear under the bridge and downstream until I couldn't see her anymore was a scene indelibly imprinted in my memory. I started crying as I walked slowly toward the house. In French, I uttered to myself, "Le, J'ai puis de Mama," which translated, "Now, I have no more Mama." I was the most heartbroken little boy in all of St. Genevieve, maybe all of the Province of Quebec!

I must have blanked out for a while because I don't remember anything until I saw my water-soaked mom walking back toward the house with my little wet friend. She had him by the hand and he was crying. The boy must have been heavy to pull out of the water, as he was wearing a thick winter coat. My mom was a strong swimmer. She had to be, to be able to pull at least forty pounds of boy with another probably five pounds of water out of a raging river. In my perception, then and now, my mom is the bravest mom I could have ever had.

I don't remember where the other twin went. He might have gone home. My mom, the boy and I walked to take him home. My mom knocked on the door and the twins' mother opened it. She looked at my mom and then at her son, drenched and cold. She then grabbed her son, yanked him inside the house and slammed the door. No thank you, no questions as to what happened . . . nothing but SLAM!

At first I remember being a bit perplexed at her reaction. It's pretty amazing how perceptive a four and a half year-old can be. I had figured that she was so mad at my mom for not watching her boy closer as he played in our yard by the river that my mom deserved what she got, and that was to be all wet and cold. I was just very happy that I got my mom back, and that's all that mattered to me!

To sum up my dad's character is a bit more complex, and requires a couple of events.

My dad had bought a shoe repair shop in Cartierville, near Montreal. I must have been four years old then. We lived upstairs from the shop in a small two-story building. There was a famous amusement park called Parc Belmont (Belmont Park) that was within walking distance. A day that will stand out in my memory with my dad was when he took me to that park. It was just he and I! We walked from the shoe shop, crossed the bridge over the Prairies River separating us from the wonderful things that were happening there. We had a wonderful father-and-son day. I remember us holding hands as we walked across the bridge. We held hands the entire time we were together.

I found the shoe shop on Google Maps just in time because now, six months later, it shows that it has been torn down. There's a Google Maps top view of it in the picture section.

My dad wasn't into rides, so we went to see the sideshows. In one of the tents was one of two giants that my dad had made shoes for. I had seen this giant come into our shop. He had to bend down in order to walk around inside. I remember getting into one of his shoes and sitting down inside it. My mom took a picture of this, but I can't find it today.

There was a black man there that could walk on the blade of a saw he had clamped in a vice. The saw's teeth were sticking upward and were digging into his feet as he walked on it. This really impressed those French Canadians, and me too—of course, I was one of them also. This African warrior was scantily dressed with what looked like a grass skirt and had painted his face with red lines that made him look really mean and scary. His hair was in a huge afro, all spread out and scraggly. There were "oohs" and "ahs" as he stomped the bottoms of his feet against the upright blade teeth. He made loud sounds like he was angry and it scared me.

My dad must have made shoes for him also, but with feet so tough, what would he ever need shoes for, except for keeping them warm as he walked out onto Canadian ice in the winter? After his show he met with my dad and they talked to each other. What appeared to be an angry savage, a black warrior with no qualms about cutting you into pieces and eating you, turned out to be a very gentle man. He spoke with my dad about how his feet really didn't hurt dancing on the edges of saw blades because of the huge calluses on the soles, and that all the yelling and hollering was just to scare little kids like me.

My dad made friends easily and everyone liked him, especially his little boy. He was my hero! Interestingly, my son has said this about me. What a joy that was to hear. However, my son is the one that turned out to be my hero, after being decorated for bravery during his tour in Afghanistan, but that's another story.

On a different note, my dad was also a playful rascal. I never heard any problems between my parents about infidelity and if there was, my mom would have found out in no uncertain terms and all hell would have broken loose. But . . . to describe my dad as an angel would not be a fair assessment. I debated whether to add this event or not, but it's about openness, and this is one of the best examples of my dad's sense of character, and a character he was.

One Sunday afternoon we had guests visit our house on the lake. There were about five couples. My parents' friends were all very fun and relaxed people. Many of them had gone swimming in the lake, which was a bit murky at times. The bottom of the lake was muddy and you didn't want to open your eyes underwater. It was a great fishing lake, but not the cleanest of water for swimming.

My mom had connected a hose to an outside spigot for guests to wash off after their swim. Dad saw that the girls were having a bit of difficulty rinsing off the lake water using one hand to operate the hose and the other hand to do a little scrubbing, so, what does a playful Frenchman do? He goes to assist the girls by hosing them off. Dad could get a little frisky after a few beers. As he was hosing them off he began hosing one particular female in certain body parts that, well, let's say were what one would consider as private. Apparently this girl and Dad got along because she made like she didn't want him to point his hose in that direction, but then again, she wasn't moving away. I think they liked each other.

What was so special about my mom and dad? Really nothing, except that for me, they were truly special!

CHAPTER 2

A CURIOSITY ABOUT LIFE

"Why do certain mountain climbers want to climb Mount Everest?"
And the typical answer was, "Because it's there!"

BEING THAT BOTH MY PARENTS HAD A THIRST FOR KNOWL-
edge, it's no wonder that I inherited such an inquisitive mind.
Ever since I can remember, I've asked the question, "Why am I
here?" When I was eight to ten years old, living in Geauga Lake, Ohio and
attending Aurora Grade School, which, by the way, had superb teachers,
I developed the idea that everything that was happening around me was
all only for me, and that there was nothing outside my existence. In other
words, I was the only true existence and all else was manifested around
me only because I was there. If I went away, everything else would also go
away. In a sense, this is true because within our thought world, the universe inside our knowledge bubble is actually all that exists to us. Knowing
that there are pyramids in Egypt, or penguins on Antarctica without ever
going there, is knowledge by evidence. Knowing that there is a building
on 39th Street and that building gets torn down without your knowledge,
that knowledge remains, but the evidence no longer exists. Which set of
circumstances is real; is it the thought world or the physical world? Both
maintain an identical validity but in different environments.

Consciousness, or self-awareness, is one reality and our three-dimensional
existence is another. Defining between the two, separating the two realities,
we can say that the reality of thought is one and the reality of matter is

another. In the non-physical realm, reality comprises only of thought. In our physical state, the perception of reality consists of a combination of the two. This can be exemplified by the fact that atheists believe that one is born, lives, and after they're dead there's nothing. In this case, their belief is that their reality in fact does go away for them. The combination of their thought and the matter around them no longer exists. For the person that believes in an afterlife, the idea that we live on after death releases us from the bonds of physical matter, but does not relinquish the idea that we can still think.

Many of today's intelligentsia is of the mindset that all learned and recorded perceptions of what's been around us from birth is who we are up to the present. They believe nothing else on the planet or in the universe enters our mental archive but through our senses and gets deposited somewhere in our brains. Many religious and spiritual people believe that when we are born into the world, after we die, if we were good we go to heaven and if we were bad we are punished forever thereafter without much regard as to how this all takes place. Their belief is based on faith. People that have had a near-death experience contend that we come into this world with so much more. They report that we have certain knowledge taken away when we come here by way of physical birth, add our experience to our non-physical knowledge bubble and recombine all this experience after we leave. They say that our purpose here is a more exciting and rewarding gift than one can ever imagine.

I write this book with conviction and what I believe is empirical evidence. I vacillated between atheist and agnostic for about thirty-five years prior to delving wholeheartedly at this quest for an answer as to why we are here and what happens to us after we die. It was my mother's passing that urged me to start searching intently for an answer to, "Where's my mom and dad?"

For five and a half years I perused the Internet for veridical experiences of people's near-death experiences. I only wanted to view experiences from credible people, like doctors and ambulance paramedics; people that were not related to the person having the near-death experience. I was not interested in the stories of heaven, dead relatives and angels that the person saw when they had temporarily died. I didn't believe that what they saw in some tunnel, or visitations by dead relatives was real, real in the sense that it had the validity of consequences. Like Susan Blackmore, a NDE critic, I believed that these visions of a tunnel, light at its end and seeing angels was part of the dying process of the brain.

Evidence began to mount that people having near-death experiences just may be for real. It reminded me of my experiences with astral projection and the three times I had an out-of-body experience. During my atheist/agnostic period, I literally had to keep reminding myself that one could actually have consciousness outside their bodies because it happened to me. It's like memory that one forgets and has to be reminded again. The video that clinched it for me that this possibility was in fact worth the effort to comprehensively study was a movie by the BBC titled *The Day I Died*. This video can be viewed on YouTube. My interest was further piqued when people that I knew personally began to speak about their experiences after I mentioned that I was very interested in this subject.

I've learned much more beside the clear evidence that there is another side to this physical life. I've learned that we have basically a singular purpose for being here. Not that we don't have multiple personal goals, ambitions and things we wish to accomplish; it simply means that there is an underlying purpose for life itself, and that includes all life, from humans to microbes, and yes, Fido too.

What's the answer, the real purpose? It's actually quite simple. But, I'm not going to reveal its utter simplicity right away. The pages of this book will provide a plausible answer. For me, it's the correct one. There's one phrase that basically sums it up. And, it's my innate hunch that you will draw your own conclusions in a way that satisfies your particular, individual paradigm of life. That does not mean that reading this book will leave you with only more questions, that you will not get at least some logical answer to the meaning of life or anything of the sort; not at all. I believe that by studying many of the experiences of people that have been to the other side that they have in fact been exposed to part of, or perhaps even the full, meaning of life. One of the challenges they have after coming back is that they have great difficulty articulating it. In fact, many that try to express what they experienced say that it's ineffable—that many aspects that they encountered can't be described in words. Not all get an answer to it, but collectively, there is a picture that emerges.

Ironically, being alive here on Earth is not much different from the old Monty Python movie, *The Meaning of Life*, and the hilarious, but often paradoxically expressed situations presented in that film. Understanding the meaning of life does not provide some sagely certificate qualifying one that they now know why they're here, that they can relax and watch it like a movie. In fact, knowledge that God exists and that there is another side has had an opposite effect on me. This revelation exposed to me the clarity and the beauty of living everyday inside each fascinating and unexpected circumstance, good to bad. It has given me solace in the face of tragic events. We will all someday have to face tragedy, and for some of us, tragedies that we have already faced. It provides an answer as to why children suffer horrible diseases, why wars are fought and people suffer unspeakable horrors.

It also provides logical answers to questions like why God, if He's love and goodness, allows such deplorable conditions to exist. It provides a reason why, for the most part, religion has been at the heart of approximately 246,000 people killed during the Crusades of the Middle Ages and the Spanish Inquisition. Why, in the past hundred years 151,491,000 have been killed over opposing beliefs. And why the regimes of Nazi Germany and Nationalist China alone have killed 141,160,000 people. And, why we die at all. On the other hand, it also reveals that life in this physical existence pushes our personal envelopes to exercise love.

This work reveals why artificial intelligence can never achieve self-awareness to any degree. Many scientists and researchers in artificial intelligence have surmised that the brain is an electro-chemical machine with billions of connections, and that if enough connections are made in a computing device, this machine will develop self-awareness. This sounds perfectly logical. However, there's a conundrum in the theory.

We will also look into the quantum world, the realm of the very small, even into multi-dimensional realms where space and time folds into itself, where mathematical possibilities allow for instantaneous travel to any portion of the universe. Here lies the mathematical and empirical evidence of laws that are extremely strange to us non-physicist types, yet this bizarre landscape offers a support structure for the existence of non-physical life in the form of nothing more than thought. An example of the strange nature of the quantum world, without getting into its details, is illustrated in the famous Schrödinger's cat *gedanken* experiment, which literally means "thought experiment." This is where he attempts to explain the nature of uncertainty by saying that a cat is both dead and alive until one opens the uniquely designed box to observe the cat's condition. Common sense dictates that something can be either in one condition or the other. However, in the quantum world, and in the non-physical realm, a thought or entity can exist in more than one state.

The afterlife is a thought world. It doesn't fit within the ambience of dreams where things change without reasoning in nonsensical fashion. It's a place where anything imaginable can be manifest into its own reality, yet it has logic, structure and organization.

Could my mom and dad be residing in such a non-physical existence, able to see and experience things so wondrous and unimaginable to us that their physical lives paled in comparison? I believe that there are many people that have been to such a place, and have come back to tell their minute portion of an infinitely vast existence where anything and everything is possible by the mechanism of the mere process of thought. The last words that Steve Jobs uttered was, "Oh wow . . . oh wow . . . oh wow!" What did Steve see that was so fantastic for him to utter this expression?

Thought *is* life. In my opinion, it's not so much that René Descartes said, "I think, therefore I am," but rather, "I am, therefore I think, and with thought, I can experience and create." Both **thinking and creating** are at the heart of existence, everything from a poem, a flower arrangement, an airplane to the Big Bang, the creation of the universe itself.

So, where are my mom and dad? There is an answer!

CHAPTER 3

WHO AM I?

WE ALL HAVE A STORY. YOUR STORY IS OF COURSE VERY different from mine. Think of your story, how you grew up, the house you lived in, your parents, relatives and friends. What teachers influenced you and how? Who was the brat in the neighborhood? What stood out as events to remember, or events you wish you could forget? All of our life's stories are being stored. Every tiny detail of every thought we've ever had is being recorded somewhere. The majority of people that have had a near-death experience have a life review, and this review is presented in exquisite detail; not so much from our visual sense that we understand it to be, but from a panoramic, 360-degree view. It includes not only our perceptions and feelings, but the perceptions and feelings of those we've been in contact with, to a second, third, fourth tier and more of people that were affected by our actions.

"Who am I?" "What am I doing here?" "Is there a heaven or a hell and am I going to go to one or the other?" I've pondered these questions over and over. I would ask myself these questions from the time when I was a small boy just barely old enough to comprehend the joys and tragedies of life. I don't believe there was anything really different about me to be pondering such philosophical ideas at such a young age.

I lived in an average household with my parents and brother. I did most of my early growing up in Geauga Lake, Ohio. That community consisted of about 500 houses in about a 2.5 square mile area where the crisscrossing gravel streets were lined with small one- and two-bedroom houses. You were considered an above-average income family if you had a three-bedroom house and nearly rich of you had a two-car garage. As a family, we basically were normal with no out-of-the ordinary problems, with the small exception that my father loved his spirits. He would get paid, stop off at Nacina's bar and have a few beers, come home and have a few more beers. Of course, one might think a few beers would be just his way of winding down after a hard day working as a tool and die maker; however, my dad was five-foot six-inches short and weighed less than a keg of beer. A full keg of beer, for those who have a need to know, is 165 pounds. So a few beers inside a 135-pound man—wow!

It was only on Friday evenings that he would rant about his week at work. I believe it was mainly to impress my mom and his two sons who, at an early age, viewed him as our fearless leader. He mostly ranted about how he saved the owner of the company tons of money, or how the "Polacks" he worked with did things in odd ways that he couldn't understand. Well, that's about all I can say negative about him—no abusive behavior. He actually loved his work and always instilled a good work ethic in us boys by saying many times, "Never miss a day of work!" He would banter for a couple of hours about his bad week, and then quickly change the subject about how the "good old Lord" could make such beautiful trees that lined our street. He would often pick up his guitar, stick a smoking cigarette in his mouth and sing country and western songs with my mom adding harmony. Which was a bit comical since he had a really heavy French accent. One of his favorites was *Married By The Bible, Divorced By The Law*, a song by Hank Snow written in the 1930's. Yes, he loved my mom, and he loved his boys just as much.

A little bit more about my dad without going into a totally boring family history, like making your friends look at 1,500 baby pictures of the same kid. He was either a restless man looking for better opportunities, or he was simply looking for new adventure. He also had a rather impulsive personality. He once got fully toasted on a Friday night and, after a few French and country western songs, his emotional French genetics signaled that he was homesick for Canada. Saturday morning my brother and I woke up to find my mom packing up, that we were all heading to Montreal for a week's vacation. He didn't tell his boss and we had no opportunity to notify anyone about why we weren't going to be in school for the entire next week. We just took off! And Mom, in full support, stayed up late and got up early to make sure everything was ready to go. She even drove the car because Dad was still reeling from his usual Saturday morning hangover.

My dad had read about Arizona, that it was also called God's country. Images of the desert, the beautiful sunsets and of course, his love of cowboys and the West in general was so alluring that he quit his job, sold our house and we all moved to Phoenix, Arizona. He was sure he could find a job after he got there, since he was an excellent tool and die maker. After a couple of months of searching with no job in sight, he decided to move on to California. Of course, Mom was in faithful compliance.

We lived in California about three years when his dream of Arizona again stirred his emotions with visions of giant cacti, mountains and lots of sand. So, off to Arizona we went again. This time it was to satisfy another dream of being a restaurateur. So he purchased the Kozy Korner Kafe, yep, with three large "K's." And, yep, we had many returning black customers. At that time my French Canadian dad had no idea of the significance of the three "K's." My mom and my brother were our only waiters and I was our only dishwasher, stove-scraper and general floor-mopper. We barely made enough money to pay the rent, but it was a restaurant and that was a real perk, being able to eat big hamburgers and steaks an inch thick any time we wanted. But the good food soon grew mundane, so rather than eating well and being poor, it was back to California where my dad's old boss hired him back. And, yep, Mom did most of the packing—again.

My dad was so good at what he did that the company he worked for in California gave him the opportunity to be the tool room foreman at their Mississippi pots and pans plant. He didn't much like city life, having grown up on a farm in Canada, so he jumped at the prospect of being in a more rural environment. The company moved us and, yep, you guessed it. Mom did most of the packing—*again.*

When we first moved to Mississippi, we lived in north Jackson. My first week of school at Provine High was a bit of a shock. I sort of knew what to expect; sort of. But it was still very different from California. And, for the clean-cut buzz haircut guys and prissy-dressed southern belles who, for the first time in their lives saw a real life, long-haired California hippie in their midst, I stood out like a sore thumb. Not that my hair was that long, it wasn't. It just covered the tops of my ears and you could still see some of my neck above my collar. Sort of like a longer-haired Elvis Presley, who was, ironically, a Mississippi native from Tupelo. So-o-o, what was the big deal? I soon discovered that a few of the guys really hated me when the pretty southern gals started eyeballing the different-looking kid from California. Yes, I used to be a pretty good-looking young man, so they said.

I had owned several motorcycles in California. Dirt bike riding was one of my preferred hobbies. Other hobbies included astronomy, looking into the wonders of the tiny world of microbial life with my microscope, drawing, and science in general. I always loved physics of all sorts and still do. But it was my motorcycle experience that turned me onto Provine high school's morning entertainment. I could ride my motorcycle on the back wheel, up-shifting through the gears, going faster and faster. I rode my motorcycle to school every day. When I approached the school from the opposite side of the football field, there was a small hill just right for picking my front wheel up and beginning my show. I would ride my bike the full length of the football field on my rear wheel. I'm not sure at the time that anyone at Provine High ever saw someone do that. After a week, literally the entire school had lined up at the end of the football field to see if that crazy California hippie would flip over on his head and break his neck. I never flipped over, but I know that's what many of them were thinking . . . and some were hoping.

That was back in 1961. Today, it's awesome what the new generation of riders are doing!

CHAPTER 4

GETTING HELP FROM SOMEWHERE

My nephew is being watched over by angels that love him dearly.

IT WAS AFTER ABOUT A MONTH OF MOTORCYCLE ACROBATICS and listening to over-my-shoulder female giggles that I went to my first school assembly in the large basketball auditorium. I had made friends with three very nerdy-looking students that rode little Honda 90cc motorcycles; they were open-minded enough to hang around with me, but still not so smart they realized that befriending such an oddball could set them apart as targets for the school's bully team. Yes, bullying was alive and well even betwixt the reputation of sanctimonious civilized southern hospitality and a self-appointed team of qualified bullies.

Huck Graham, bless his heart, during the height of the assembly, walked over to me, got within nose-to-nose touching distance and said, "Get away from me, you California quar!" Now, I had no idea what a "quar" was and was quite perplexed at such an aggressive stance, especially during a school assembly. In California, civilized fighters would meet after school in the parking lot of Lucky's supermarket and engage in their bout of fisticuffs over some legitimate difference.

What had I done to this 240 pound, six-foot whale of a boy to offend him so much? After all, I was only five-foot-nine and weighed a soaking wet 135 pounds. So, I backed up to get away from him. He came at me a second time with a fierce, "I said, get away from me, you California quar!" Complying with his command, I backed up again. When he did this a third time, what does a California infiltrator do? He acts out his most ferocious, fiery, furious bluff just so he has a chance to survive another day.

I grabbed him by the collar of his shirt, yanked him to my level, about a full head and a half downward, and stuck my forefinger in his face like a scolding mother. Then I repeated, "I'm going to kick your ass, I'm going to kick your ass, I'm going to kick your ass!" That shocked him, for about fifteen full seconds. I guess he'd never had anyone say that to him, maybe because of his sheer gigantic size. I thought for sure I had just saved my life with the biggest, baddest bluff I'd ever done or seen.

I quickly discovered that bluffing yourself out of a fight had not been instilled into Mississippi culture! He lunged at me like an angry eight-year-old girl that just had her favorite doll stolen by the neighborhood thief. All I could see were flinging arms and flailing fists coming at me like a runaway freight train. My friends said later that there was steam coming out of his ears. Unfortunate for the locomotive was that I had been studying martial arts for nearly five years and knew better than to face an angry cyclopean straight on. Having a terrific back kick then (I would fall on my ass if I tried this today), I defended myself with its snap right into his groin area. His pants split from his belt down to his knee, exposing his underwear for all to see.

Those good-ole southern boys don't take a likin' to havin' their skivvies exposed in any sort of public place, let alone right in front of their sidekicks and, of course, the ladies. I think I actually saw a dagger come out of one of his eyes. He backed up, recomposed, and proceeded to unbutton his shirt and quickly removed it—I guess so it wouldn't be spattered all over with my blood. He lunged at me again. This time with hands outstretched looking to wring my neck like a chicken—literally! I figured he was expecting that snapping back kick again, so, instead, I turned my back to him, like I'd been trained, and waited for the chugging locomotive to arrive. When he got there, I simultaneously reached downward and rearward, grabbing hold of whatever I could fit in my clenching fist, and with my other hand, over my opposite shoulder, grabbing whatever it found up there. With his own momentum, having a really big package in the palms of my hands, there was no other direction for him to go but with the force of gravity, face down, with as much added pulling force as my adrenaline-infused body could muster.

Ker-clunk!

I quickly thought, *I can't let him up, or this will be the day I find out if there's life after death!* I couldn't find a shot at him that would effectively put him out. He had his head facing the floor and, for some strange reason, he just laid there. Had he tried to get up, I could have gotten a useful shot, but instead, he just lay there—moaning, his mouth muffled in the crux of his elbow. So, what was the second best, or worst, thing to do to a gargantuan, horizontal monolith that just tried to kill you, lying on the floor with his nose against the tile? You punch him in the back of the head, right? No, incorrect answer. You will break the bones in your hand if you do that. Which is exactly what I did.

What happened to Mr. Behemoth? Fortunately for me, when he fell, his right arm took the brunt of his entire 240 pounds and it parted right at the elbow. The ulna and radius bones of his forearm had gone half way behind his humerus bone. That was not humorous at all. After letting him up, what I saw was a terrified-looking Mr. Graham, holding his foreshortened forearm with his left hand, and his minions' jaws dropped to the floor. They must have thought, *How could this little California "quar" do this to our leader, the one chosen to protect us from "quars" and other bad elements from the outside world?*

I spent the rest of the day being eyeballed by every other tough guy in the school. I could sense that they wanted to try me out to either see if I could do that again, or intimidate me into not messing with them so they could get their chance at being the temporary school bully while Huck's arm healed.

Meanwhile, the school principal, Mr. Sessums, called the police to have me arrested. You see, Huck was one of the school's star football heroes and football season had just begun. Everyone, and I mean *everyone* in Mississippi loves football, especially Mr. Sessums. Holy crap, what had I just done to make things much, much worse than beating up the school bully? I had just extinguished any chance of Provine High School from winning their usual number of football games! And boy, let me tell you, Mr. Sessums remembered that day for years afterward. When I applied for a job with one of Jackson's most highly respected advertising agencies, I received a scathing review. It appeared that the owner of the business knew Mr. Sessums personally and when he asked if he ever heard of me, since I went to Provine years earlier, Mr. Sessums told him that I was nothing but a big troublemaker and not to hire me. I'm sure he said nothing about the police finding that Huck started it and that I merely finished it.

That evening after the big fight, while recalling the story of the day, there came a bang, bang, bang on the front door. The three little friends that were with me during the kerfuffle had followed me home. They looked at each other in one of those uh-oh moments and then over at me. They looked like they were about to see Huck barge into our living room with pistols blazing, shooting everyone in sight. My mom and dad looked so scared, and my instinct was to protect them even with my life! I said, "I need to take care of this myself, I'm responsible." With a bit of trepidation, I went to the door, slowly cracking it just to see how many of Huck's friends I would be facing with a broken bone in my best hand to defend myself. Puzzled, I only saw Huck! He was standing there with his right arm in a tight sling draping over his shoulder. When I opened the door a little more, he smiled, stretched out his huge left hand upside down and said, "I want to shake the hand of a man!" So, with my right hand to his upside down left hand, we shook and became very good friends. Now, that's a man!

I wondered what had really happened that day. Was that just a lucky happenstance that I wasn't beat to a pulp, or possibly actually killed? Even though I had been studying Shotokan Karate in California, it's pretty well known that this style of karate is not favored for protecting yourself in a street fight. I studied the art of it because it was fun. I never entertained the idea that I would ever need it to defend myself. My sensei (teacher) may have sensed that I was not the fighting type, because as everyone in the class was advancing, for some reason, I was being held back. Also, for that matter, this was only the second fight I'd ever been in, so I had literally no experience in the real deal. The first one was with one of my best friends, Randy Shull, and it wasn't even what I would call a fight, but rather a shoving match with a couple of whizzing misses and only one connection—again, mine. And again, I was outweighed by nearly fifty pounds. My friend Randy was at least three inches taller too. I've always had the feeling that someone or something was watching over me during that incident also. The fact that I didn't have my lights put out was, for me, proof that, in my recollection of this and other things, there are interventions from some source other than what we perceive is our reality. Maybe I'm wrong on this, but then again, what if I'm right?

Wrong or right, there's much more evidence of what I simply can't dismiss as pure chance and that we all have spirit guides or some guiding force watching over our activities. The following are more examples of what I have always believed were further interventions that support my beliefs. I've talked to several people about near tragedies and many have said very similar things; that they had brushes with some events they felt their guardian angel had something to do with it.

Not getting my clock cleaned in a couple of confrontations is one thing, but I can't explain why I had survived the following.

I was riding my Harley at my usual near-wide-open throttle when I rounded a blind curve. Right at the final tangent where I could see the road straightened out were four cows just standing there right in the middle of the road. What in the world they were doing there made no sense to me. There was no grass to eat and the road was certainly hard on their feet. Yes, I know cows have hooves, but at the time, coming from California, cows had "feet." All I could do was hit the brakes, but I was going much too fast to come to a stop before colliding with the girls. The rear tire locked up with a loud screech and my front brake was as tight as I could squeeze the lever on the handle bar. I was sure that there would be milk and blood all over the road by the time the coroner arrived to pick up my dead, broken body.

Then, just like Moses parting the Red Sea, two cows went toward one side of the road and two went to the other side, leaving just enough space for me and my bike to squeeze between them at about forty miles per hour with my rear tire still screeching. My roll bar hit the hind leg of one of the cows and bent around my calf (no, I didn't haven a baby cow riding with me, this was my lower leg). Luckily this didn't knock my bike off balance and send me careening down the street, leaving pizza-looking skin all over my body, or again, possible death. As soon as I had passed through the bovine breach, I released my brakes, downshifted and pulled over to the side of the road. When I looked back, those stupid cows had reconvened right back where they were, in the middle of the road. I can only figure that I had some help with this.

Another time I was riding home on a rural road that I had used hundreds of times. I knew this road like the back of my hand, so there was no reason for me to slow down since I had never slowed down before. There was a slight incline before a set of railroad tracks that I loved to hit at around seventy miles per hour because it catapulted me off the ground, jumping over the tracks all together. That was always a thrill. Flashlights are measured in candlepower, and the headlight on my Harley could also be measured using this method. The difference is that I think a single candle might have lit up the road better than its headlight.

It was common in those rural parts of Mississippi not to have those motorized railroad-crossing gates. There weren't even crossing lights or reflectors at this intersection. Not that a little reflector would have even worked with my abysmal headlight. All they had installed was a big black and white striped "X" on the side of the road to indicate that it was a railroad crossing. It was pitch dark! There was no moonlight, not even starlight because it was overcast. I couldn't see more than ten to fifteen yards ahead of my front wheel and was looking forward to making the Flying Wallenda jump across the railroad tracks. For some totally unexpected reason, this night I hit my brakes some thirty yards before the tracks. To this day, I have no idea why I did this because, like I said, I had never done it before! What I heard then scared the bejesus out of me. It was a freight train crossing the road. Had I kept the throttle on so I could make my flying leap over the tracks, the only thing that could have saved me was going through two open doors of a boxcar, like something you might see in one of those old black and white Charlie Chaplin movies. I had some help from somewhere on this one for sure!

And yet another time I was dirt bike riding with my 1971 Husqvarna 400 CC Cross when I decided I would climb a gnarly hill I'd seen earlier that day. What a real show-off does at the top of one of these hills, should he even make it to the top, is keep going on the rear wheel to show that he's in total control of his element. This is what I *always* did after conquering a rutted, whoop-de-doo dirt wall-looking hill climb. But . . . this time I didn't do it. If I had needed to take a dump, I would have unloaded in my leathers because the top of the hill had barely one bike length before it dropped off straight down, at least fifty feet, into a rock quarry where earthmovers had been excavating. I swear by the hair on my chinny-chin-chin, half of the rubber on my front tire was on the ground and the other half was hanging over the emptiness of the abyss. What if I had decided not to put on my brakes and do what a red-blooded, young and stupid show-off always did in the past? Believe me when I say again, I had some help from somewhere!

Recently I was sitting at an intersection in my Nissan van waiting for my light to turn green. When a traffic light turns from red to green it's the normal thing for anyone that drives in America to push on the gas pedal and proceed through the intersection. I looked to my right and left as I always do, but this time I didn't go forward. I just sat there! Then, like only an idiot or a drunk would do, this car comes flying through the intersection from the turning curb lane, past the stopped cars in the two middle lanes at what I estimate was at least fifty miles per hour! I couldn't believe my eyes that bozos like this inhabited our planet, or that they made it to an age where a driver's license was issued. He flew past the nose of my Nissan, missing me by inches. Had I moved forward when the light turned green, I would surely have been killed from this crash! Yes, I truly believe that I had some assistance of mental delay from somewhere!

I'm sure you've had some incident in your life that you can recall where it appeared that it was more than just chance that saved your butt.

Back in Mississippi, my dad had retired and built his dream house on beautiful Lake Cavalier north of Jackson. He built his dream houseboat by himself there too, and sat in his favorite chair with his favorite beer in his hand. He would sit on his favorite front porch where he could watch his favorite wife, my mom, go back and forth, back and forth, mowing the acre of their beautiful front yard. He told me that these were the happiest days of his life. My dad used to mow the lawn, but Mom stopped him from doing this. He wouldn't use the push mower; that was too much work. He used the small tractor mower for convenience.

One day he was mowing with the tractor mower when the entire tractor flipped over on top of him as he was trying to cut the grass in a deep ditch. The throttle was on a small dash panel and when it flipped, the engine kept running for a few minutes. Mom saw what had happened and recounted that the blades of the mower were inches from Dad's face. Dad was pinned and couldn't move. Mom said that it could have sliced his face to bits. Was this another case of intervention?

These events pale in comparison to my nephew's experiences. I believe he's either one of the luckiest people I know, or he's being watched over by angels that love him dearly.

There's a place here in the South Bay of the Los Angeles area called Sunken City. It's where the ocean meets the cliffs, which are constantly being reformed from the effects of coastal erosion and seismic activity in that area. There are short portions of old roads atop jutting spires and the continuation of the same road some thirty feet below it. It's literally a sunken city. My son was in his late teens and my nephew was in his early twenties when they went for a local Friday night's gathering of like-minded peers. The teenagers would go to Sunken City to light campfires, light up conversation and light up a doobie or two.

The town of San Pedro, where Sunken City is located, also had its bad element. A group of gang members showed up, maybe to put claim on the territory that was occupied with mostly middle-class kids. My nephew loves to make friends with new people and decided in his mind that these guys were "cool." He may not have recognized the M13 tattoos in the middle of their foreheads or that they just didn't speak with the eloquence of the rest of the crowd, who, by the way, dispersed when they showed up. My son's skateboard was immediately confiscated by the ruffians, whereupon he promptly left. My nephew may not have seen that altercation and remained long enough to be pitched off the edge of a two hundred-foot precipice.

He left the earth, airborne, and luckily glanced off a large boulder feet-first, down to another boulder, to hit a switchback path where he was falling much too fast to stop. He kept flying, doing a three hundred sixty degree flip hitting another boulder onto the same switchback path, feet-first again and still falling too fast to stop. He hit some more boulders and the same switchback a third time and again, falling too fast to stop, he continued where he came to rest on the beach sand two hundred-some feet from where he started—*on his feet*. But folks, that's not all!

The gang members, probably thinking they had killed him, broke into his van, pulling out his key tumbler in an attempt to steal it by hotwiring it. My nephew had had trouble with the key tumbler and they were not able to get the van started. It took my nephew a very long time to get back to his van, as it was not possible to climb back up the cliff from whence he came. So, the long arduous climb around the point of the cliffs began. When he got to his van, the ruddy rat pack had left after vandalizing his possessions. What the hoods didn't know was that to start his van, my nephew would stick a screwdriver in his key tumbler just where only he knew how to do it.

He stuck the key tumbler back into the steering column, stuck his screwdriver in the tumbler, started his van and drove off. He entered the freeway onramp when his screwdriver and key tumbler fell out of the hole and locked his steering wheel in place at 45 miles per hour, in a turn, with a caravan of traffic on his tail! He slammed on his brakes, skidded to one inch of hitting the concrete barrier, completely out of the way of traffic behind him and without a scratch on his van. What was that evening all about?

I could tell many more stories where this lucky soul cheated death, but I'll only include two more. He was pulling his toy-hauler-type trailer filled with motorcycles when the traffic in front of him abruptly stopped. He slammed on him brakes, but had not plugged his electric brake wires to his trailer. His van tires screeched while the mass of his full trailer continued to push him forward as if he had no brakes at all. Right at the point where he was about to rear-end the car in front of him, his van veered off to the left, missing the car! He came to a stop a few car lengths ahead of a serious lawsuit, and worse, possible injury, or even, God forbid, getting his ass beat by the driver of the car he just missed. He was in the oncoming lane of traffic and, as luck or some divine intervention would have it, no cars were coming head on.

And lastly, one day he was riding his skateboard catty-corner through an intersection, directly in front of a cop. The poor guy had no ID on him and the cop took him directly to jail. Now my nephew is quite small in stature and can say the darnedest things. We don't know what he said in there, but he was harassed by the inmates and left the jail the next day with nothing but his pants and underwear. Yes, they took his shoes and socks too! But for the most part, he was in good physical shape.

My nephew has had many of these types of incidents that would make for an interesting autobiography. He's very intelligent. He's also a high functioning autistic with Asperger's Syndrome, attention deficit disorder, and was born with no kneecaps—that's called Nail Patella Syndrome. He lives in the parking lot of my building, in his toy-hauler with his black cat, Maverick. He reads his Bible every day, and I believe he's had *lots* of help!

CHAPTER 5

GROWING UP A BIT, AND RETURNING HOME

That was my first realization of a deep-felt experience of true unconditional love!

I WENT TO NINE DIFFERENT SCHOOLS MY LAST FOUR YEARS OF high school. We had lived in various towns and cities in Canada, Rhode Island, Massachusetts, Arizona, California and Mississippi, where my dad finally passed away with the mindset that the "good ole Lord" was going to take care of him. With all his searching for that place of contentment, his house on the lake in Mississippi fulfilled his earthly dream. His last move was totally up to the "good ole Lord." Last count, we had moved thirty-seven times.

I have to add that moving thirty-seven times and going to nine different high schools didn't psychologically affect me one iota. One small challenge that did change my life occurred in the last house I lived in with my parents. This was when we moved from Jackson to Flora, Mississippi, where the high school's graduating class consisted of four kids. I dearly wanted to be a brain surgeon and had been taking physiology, chemistry and Latin, along with other academic classes my California high school counselor had suggested for my doctorate. When I showed my new Mississippi counselor, who was also the principal (and the coach, math teacher and maintenance custodian) my curriculum, he told me that he could give me Biology 2 over again and give me credit for it. They had no one there that taught Latin, chemistry or any other courses that would allow me to further my education toward being a doctor, let alone a brain surgeon. Also, since I was in Mississippi, I was required to take Mississippi history in order to graduate.

What? I had already taken Ohio history in order to graduate, California history in order to graduate, Arizona history in order to graduate, and now I was a senior in high school to be placed in a class of ninth graders to learn all about the history of Mississippi? For heaven's sake, I knew I wasn't going to live there the rest of my life. I'm a French Canadian with one-eighth Algonquin Indian blood in me. I was genetically predisposed to explore. That's when I packed up my bow and arrow and quit high school to carve my own path in what I then viewed as this unfair and cruel world I had grown to perceive. That's just how the young and stupid do it, right? "Screw it," I thought, "I'm on my own!" I was getting frustrated at so little to do living in a small town of just a couple hundred people.

So, I left Flora, Mississippi to move into the big city, Jackson, twenty miles away. There I would find a job, make lots of money, buy a new motorcycle and live happily ever after. How else would a frustrated seventeen-year-old boy think? Since I had made a few friends (and a few enemies) at Provine High School, I contacted my friend Tommy to see if he knew anyone that had a place for me to stay. Tommy told me about someone that might be looking for a roommate. What he didn't tell me was that John was gay. What happens when a fairly good-looking, delusional boy of seventeen meets a thirty-seven-year-old gay guy? The gay guy falls in love, the seventeen-year-old boy runs away and the gay guy shoots himself. Yes, John shot himself and died shortly after my four-week stay. I was never sure why he shot himself; was it because he couldn't deal with being gay in a mostly anti-gay community? Or was it that I didn't want him as a room-mate, or that he was not able to deal with rejection? Bless his heart, he was a very nice person, compassionate and caring—just not my type.

I sometimes think of where John might be, and because of this inci-dent, I have looked into near-death experiences of gay people that have committed suicide. Their experiences don't appear to be any different from any other. Gay people return with experiences of having been uncondition-ally loved. For example, one particular incident was of a young gay man named Martin who committed suicide alone in his room. He overdosed on prescription pills. His mother found him and called paramedics. He was taken to one hospital, and then flown by helicopter to a better-equipped one because of his serious condition. He was in the helicopter when he felt that he was going to die; he flat-lined in flight. He then saw that he was in a room; he found himself to be absolutely perfect, rejuvenated, dressed in the most pure, cleanest white he'd ever seen. He was looking down at his own body. He also found himself talking with his deceased grandmother, who had been very religious. He was pleased at the fact that even though his grandmother had not approved of his gay lifestyle when she was alive, he felt her love, love for just who he was. She then left the room and he wanted to go with her, but he was held back, rooted to the ground as if he couldn't move his feet. After this, he found himself back in his body. He had survived.

The doctors said he was going to have brain damage because he was out for so long. They also said he was going to have organ damage and that he would not be able to walk again. After a full recovery, his mother showed him a text message he had sent to her and several friends before his suicide attempt. It was a simple, "I love you." He said that everyone to whom he had sent that message replied with, "I love you too." His realization from this experience was that he was not alone! The outcome and the full recovery were most surely that he had help.

Another testimony of a gay man admits he hated himself for being addicted to drugs. In December of 1979, he found what he thought was cocaine, but that he had actually snorted a half gram of PCP, which is enough to kill several people. A friend found him and called the paramedics. In his near-death state he came into the presence of a white light. When he looked at his body, it was as if he could see through it. It was then that he realized he must be dead. His recollection was that he felt that he was loved. He also felt that there was no sense of time. He was in the presence of knowledge. He had a life review where he saw everything he had ever experienced, but with no judgment. He did not like what he saw during this review; everything from his viewpoint was negative.

When this was over, he found himself back in his body. He then began manifesting voices taking over his body. This went on for about three days. The hospital's doctor attempted to place him in the psychiatric ward. His family fought to keep him out. They brought him home where he was introduced to their church. He is now a Christian. His life has totally changed, with no desire for drugs. After several years of not knowing his condition of HIV, he was tested and was found to be positive for AIDS, but is surviving. His life now entails working with others in his ministry. He's alive today because he believes that he had help.

Dr. Ian Stevenson studied more than 3,000 cases over a forty-year period of children that experienced a past life. These studies revealed a possible reason as to why people have an opposite gender identity. Cases of young girls that remember being a man in a past life will sometimes prefer men's clothing and have interests that are more masculine. The opposite is also true. Young boys that remember being a female will have a penchant for feminine things and possess a feminine persona.

This begs the question; is being gay a choice or is gender something over which we are not in control?

For almost a year I lived with various friends in Jackson. Mom had no idea where I was. I never called and never went back home to live with my parents. Years later she told me that she would imagine me walking up the street, toward the house, across our front yard and through the front door. That didn't happen for a painfully long time. Kids can be so cruel without knowing what they may be doing to cause others pain. Hearing this from my mom, even so long afterward, was both touching and heartbreaking. I know that the son she loved so dearly was missed and the thought of not knowing where that son was, dead or alive, haunted her immensely. She knew that I rode my motorcycle at ninety miles an hour everywhere I went. What else could she have been thinking? What am I going to experience in my own life review? I've cried many times thinking of my mom and how much she loved me. I've also cried often thinking of my dad hugging his boys and remembering how hard he worked to provide a good and comfortable life for his family.

After wandering around, living here and there in Jackson, still searching for my head, I decided to go to Canada, my roots, where my homies might understand me a little better than the people of Mississippi—so I thought. I felt a bit like a fish out of water in Mississippi. It wasn't a bad place to live. It was more like moving to another country with a different culture. But it was the same country; it was just a very different culture. At first, I was not accustomed to the southern style. After having lived there for fifteen years, I began to understand that living in the Deep South was more about politeness, integrity and Christian values. In the 1960's, the south was changing and many southerners were not keen to have their southern hospitality and charm slowly eroded by having those "nawtheners" as neighbors that don't wave or smile. They didn't want or feel that they needed any "damn Yankees" that stood in line at the bank without saying a word to the person they were standing next to. I met many wonderful people there. What's not well known is that even though Mississippi is the poorest state, it gives more to charity per capita than any other state in the Union! I often tell people I'm from the south, even though it's actually south Canada, but in my mind, it's perfectly okay that I'm viewed as a southerner.

I made a quick visit home where my mom thought about my decision and got me a train ticket to Montreal to stay with some relatives until my head was screwed back on straight. I got on the train for Canada in Jackson. Between the Jackson station and the Chicago station, maybe somewhere in Tennessee or Kentucky, a very nicely dressed, very conservative-looking woman was walking down the aisle. She slowly passed me, then turned around, came back, bent down close to my face and said, "What did you say?" I said, "I didn't say anything." She then said, "You said I had a nice ass." I was horrified! "No, I didn't say anything at all! I would never say anything like that." She then quietly said, "You know, a woman really likes to be complimented about her ass, and that was a very nice compliment." I continued to adamantly deny saying anything, because saying something like that was totally out of character for me. After all, I had been living in the south, and had learned how to treat a lady. She kept insisting that I said it, and that she was very appreciative of the compliment. I kept denying it! Boy, was I naïve. I was clueless about her motives. She asked if she could sit next to me since that seat was empty. Even after a while, I still thought I was in some sort of trouble; that she was going to call the conductor and have me thrown off the train.

She was maybe in her late twenties or early thirties, although when you're eighteen, someone that age has the appearance of being much older than you are. She had black hair and wore butterfly shaped glasses suspended by a little chain that went around her neck. She was a schoolteacher living in Chicago. I thought she was very pretty for a woman that old. We talked the afternoon away and I could tell that she really liked me. I just didn't realize how much until dinnertime.

She invited me to sit with her in the dining car and have dinner together. She began drinking wine and convinced the waiter that I was old enough to drink. She got more and more tipsy and kept buying drinks for both of us. On top of tipsy, she began to get frisky and then, downright horny. She pulled her black trousers down below her crotch revealing her white underwear. I was very impressed that she would do this right in the dining car. She was the coolest teacher I had ever met!

I now have the distinction of having been molested by a schoolteacher because later that evening, we quietly went to our seats and under a blanket, I was very politely attacked! I have to admit that I had no inkling of turning this teacher into the police after such a memorable experience. I was not psychologically damaged in any way from this. But it was nuts! I don't know if I had any sort of help with this one. I'll just chalk this one up as an experience to bring back with me after I'm in heaven. I hope I get to see her again over there under very different circumstances.

Conversely, my dad had an opposite experience when he was about ten years old. He was molested by his Catholic priest and remained angry about this event for the rest of his life. This was in 1924. In 2002, the Boston Globe published documents where the Catholic church had been protecting priests from the law. In America more than 450 priests and bishops had resigned after this investigation. The movie, "Spotlight" tells the story of the Catholic church covering up this behavior.

I bring these incidents up because many people have a stigma about sex. I don't happen to have that gene. It overlooked me when I arrived as a sperm and met my other half, the egg. I'm not promiscuous, I'm not gay, I'm not perverted; however, I've always been sexually charged. In my studies of near-death experiences, one NDE'er mentioned that God isn't interested in your sex life. What she meant by this is that sex is not on his list of do's and don'ts. However, the act of sex coupled with the intent of hurting someone purely for your self-gratification is a different issue. After reading what this NDE'er wrote, I told myself, "I'm off the hook!" What she said about her NDE was that God is more interested in how we relate with each other from the standpoint of love. I will elaborate on this later.

I moved in with my grandmother on Mom's side, on Sherbrook Street in Montreal. I learned quickly that my grandmother was not my mom. Grandma loved her spirits and had a bit of a temper. She would get on my case over little things, like inviting a friend to spend the night at her house without asking her first—yeah, little stuff like that.

I went to work for J.P Coats, a textile company where I was given the worst job in the entire company. I was making Alusil wax for treating the thread they manufactured. That job sucked, and I had one of the worst bosses of my working career; mind you, I said one of the worst. The worst boss I ever had was an engineering manager with an ego much larger than his talent. This guy didn't have a clue how to treat people. He rode my case, and quite frankly, everyone else's, the entire six months I worked for him. I quit and about two weeks after this, he was fired.

I left the job at J.P. Coats to join the Canadian Air Force where, after five weeks of basic training, I decided I wanted OUT! I had a nearly perfect record. I was a model airman and was the only one in my outfit that never got his bed tore up by the Drill Sergeant for having a wrinkle in its top blanket. What they never knew was that I never actually made the bed. I would slip under the covers from the pillow end at night and in the mornings I would slip back out the opposite way. This was a simple little trick I thought of to allow me a little extra time every morning. As the mattress sagged, the covers became loose under my weight. I would slip in like filling a taco and slip out like pulling a weenie out of a hot dog bun. The bed sheet covers conveniently sprung back tightly without one single wrinkle. For five weeks, with the exception of Saturday morning when we replaced the bed sheets, I watched all the guys struggle to make a wrinkle-free bed while I traipsed merrily into the lavatory to brush my teeth. No one ever told on me.

Nevertheless, I wanted out! Badly! The military just wasn't my thing. When the Drill Sergeant and I discussed how badly I wanted out, he suggested that I see the base psychiatrist. The psychiatrist suggested I take some sort of test. I thought it was to see if I was crazy or not. I thought of all the reasons I might be abnormal, all the schools I went to, being molested, moving thirty-seven times, watching my dog being shot by a policeman (yes, but that's another story). No, it wasn't an "are you crazy" test; it was an IQ test, and that's the second IQ test that verified that I was a genius. One of your dumber geniuses, right on the cusp with 152, but a genius nonetheless. I might add that having a high IQ doesn't hold as much value as a good EQ. This is a measure of a person's adequacy in such areas as self-awareness, empathy, and dealing sensitively with other people.

When I was put in front of the commanding officer and three other officers with all the scrambled eggs coutured into their uniforms—which is a term used by lower-ranking airmen to describe all the ornamentation and decorations on higher-ranking officer's uniforms—I got the ass reaming of my life. I had never had that sort of convoluted treatment. They gave me the harshest, downright cruel compliments I had ever experienced. It was a verbal dichotomy; fiercely yelling at the top of their lungs how great of an airman I was. They assured me that if I stayed in, I could be anything I wanted. They yelled and scolded that I would quickly rise in rank, I could have any job I chose. I could even be a pilot! Why in God's name couldn't they have said it more nicely? I might have reconsidered. After all, I only had one more week of basic training to go. Could it be that they simply had a low EQ? After basic, they said that military life gets much easier. What would I have become if I had made the decision to stay? This question is pivotal to the explanation of predestination and free will as explained in a later chapter.

I received my last paycheck, packed up my belongings, including a really cool Canadian Air Force uniform, and bought a bus ticket to California.

I lived in Huntington Park for a while working for a company called Sargent Industries. I then moved to a dinky Hollywood hotel where the manager threw me and a roommate nicknamed "Flash" out on the street. The father of a girl that I had picked up hitchhiking came into my room looking for his daughter. I had dropped her off a few blocks away, but in the process of following my car, he must not have seen that she had exited. He looked under the bed, in the closet, yelling and making a big scene. The tenants called the manager, and the father of the girl and him got into a huge shouting match. I thought they were going to physically go at it. The manager was about half the size of the father, but stood his ground and threw all three of us out. I left actually admiring the manager for what he stood for, his integrity.

With no place to stay, I decided to leave Hollywood and go to San Francisco. I became a genuine tune-in, turn-on, drop-out hippie, stoned about a third of the time on acid or whatever someone gave me, still looking for answers as to "why I'm here." This was the beginning of my awakening from hippie life. I was thrown in jail when a cop stopped me and thought I was stoned on acid. What was so ironic about this was that, this time, I wasn't stoned on anything! While I was in jail, my car and everything I owned was stolen.

I spent three days there while they checked me out. I was told that I had committed a felony. That was serious! However, the felony was added because I told them that I was born in Canada and that anyone that's not a US citizen that commits a misdemeanor had automatically committed a felony. They never told me why I was released, but my guess is that after checking into my background, they found that since I had come into the US before I was fourteen, and my parents had become US citizens, I was automatically a US citizen. They didn't pump out my stomach to find the drug so they could charge me with possession. But I wish they had—they wound have found nothing, not even food! Boy, was I hungry when I was arrested. At least I got to eat free for three days.

About a week after I was let out of jail, riots broke out on the streets of San Francisco. I could write another book about this, but to make a long story short, the National Guard picked me up off the streets. One of them jumped out of a big truck and threw me on the ground, stepped on my face to keep me from getting up, then picked me up and literally threw, I mean *threw* me about five feet through the air into a police paddy wagon. I found myself again in jail and again went before the same judge from a week earlier that had let me out on my own recognizance after being picked up by the "blue meanies" for being stoned, as I mentioned, which I was not. This time there were literally hundreds, maybe thousands more people that were arrested for being on the streets during the riots.

The judge was black, it was San Francisco, her name was Kennedy and my driver's license said I was from Mississippi. I'm lucky she didn't turn me around and send me right back to my bunk. This time I got a suspension for violating the curfew that had been imposed due to the riots. She told me that if she ever saw me again, she would put me away for a very long time.

I left the courtroom and, without a car to sleep in, ended up living homeless on the streets. After being thrown in jail twice, once for not being stoned and the other for violating a curfew imposed by the San Francisco Police Department during the riots of 1966, I decided being a hippie wasn't for me. The revelation came to me while I was actually stoned on acid on the roof of a four-story house at 1090 Page Street, a few blocks from the Psychedelic Shop in the Haight-Ashbury area. I was pretty depressed and thought of jumping off the rooftop. Life just wasn't fair!

In my heightened state of LSD-ness, as I looked out over the city, I began to marvel at the streetlights and the traffic signals that changed from green, to yellow, to red and back to green. I could see one of the bay bridges with cars going across and the sound of sirens from either fire trucks or ambulances on their way to assist someone in distress. I watched this for most of the entire night, thinking, boy, Timothy Leary was wrong, that he must be really leery! The system works no matter how you bad-mouth it. Timothy couldn't do this on his own, so who was he to tell me to tune in, turn on and drop out? My first acid trip had opened an existence for me that was outside of the reality I knew, and this last acid trip brought me to the realization that being stoned was a waste of a good brain, or at least what was left of it.

I returned to Mississippi where my mom greeted me by running out into the driveway with tears in her eyes. It was hard for me to imagine what she felt seeing the little boy she gave birth to looking like a homeless bum, wearing torn clothes with a filthy face and hands, long shaggy hair and a really scraggly beard. I was never reprimanded, but rather taken into her love, no conditions, no preaching and no put-downs. That was my first realization of a deep-felt experience of true unconditional love!

After a thorough clean up, my brother talked his boss into hiring me in the research and development department of a manufacturer that made garden equipment. I worked my way into the engineering department and, to make another very long story short, thirty-four years ago started my own company doing contract engineering and manufacturing. I take ideas and turn them into products. It's very rewarding! For a high school drop-out, I've done okay, and Mom and Dad always said that they were very proud of me, even though I think back now about how I was actually a rebellious little shit—but in doing so, I believe I had help.

CHAPTER 6

MAGIC MUSHROOMS AND THE COUNTDOWN!

10, 9, 8, 7, 6, 5, 4, 3, 2, 1 . . . I'm God!

I WAS WORKING AT MAGNA AMERICAN CORPORATION IN Raymond, Mississippi; the company where my brother helped me get a job. It was a good job. I had rented a tiny two-bedroom house and had recently married Shirley, the little sister of my best friend Tommy, and was really not interested in renewing any of my past hippie habits from the land of fruits and nuts, as we called California at the time. But the thought of experiencing something new piqued my curiosity. Some of my friends had started an underground newspaper called *The Kudzu* and had showed up at my house. They told me about a new way to get stoned. They mentioned an organic, natural way to have a spiritual experience. So, it was off into the meadows of Mississippi for some magic mushroom picking.

What's interesting about magic mushrooms is that they grow out of cow poop that's been baking in the sun after a heavy morning rain. They are unmistakable. They're a light brownish white with a little purple ring around their stems just below their umbrella tops. We waited several days for a good morning rain when lo and behold, one serendipitous Saturday it poured from the time we woke up to around noon. Then, right on schedule, around 3:00 pm the hot summer sun began to bake the pasture pastries and sure as shootin', the shrooms popped up out of the meadow muffins just like we were told they would.

45

We gathered up our large brown grocery bags and out we went, shroom pickin'. We filled three large shopping bags with the biggest, loveliest mushrooms the hot baked poop could sprout from their nutritious, bountiful composition. The conditions were absolutely perfect.

We excitedly went home, knowing that that evening would be at least interesting. It would either turn into a police raid stemming from one of our nosy neighbors watching a bunch of bobble-heads out in the yard watching the lawn grow, or turn into intellectual dialogue about all the cool colors vibrating out of our wooden floor. I invited several of my friends from *The Kudzu* who had educated me about shrooms and we began to figure out ways to eat them without throwing up. If you can keep them down for about two hours, they will offer up their mystical experience.

The cuisine of choice was boiling the shrooms in a Kool-Aid broth or a sliced-and-diced topping spread over peanut butter sandwiches. What creativity! We ate a carefully portioned amount of little shroom chunks on peanut butter sandwiches and chased them with the electric Kool-Aid. We all just sat there, looking at each other, daring not to move so that we wouldn't agitate our nauseous stomachs. We all turned green fighting back the urge to upchuck.

As the first hour passed, we kept asking, "Feel anything yet?" "Nope, nothing yet." An hour and a half passed and we were beginning to feel a bit more human as the nausea subsided. At around the hour and forty-five minute mark, the first signs of magical shroom room changes began to appear. We kept moving our fingers past our eyes, looking for trailers. For anyone that has never experienced psychedelics, trailers are residual images retained by the sensitized retinas. You can swirl your finger like a cork screw and see the retained cork screw image linger suspended in air for a few seconds and unscrew itself after you've stuck your finger in your ear—for some strange reason.

We began to hear expressions like, "Wow," "Oh, man," "Geez," "Holy cow" (maybe because of the cow poop). I was getting really buzzed. I passed a certain point where I don't remember anything about being in my living room. The only thing I can remember was that I found myself in a totally different realm that I had never experienced before. I clearly remember, even after forty-seven years, going back in time to an old wooden sailing ship. It was rocking, rolling and pitching. I remember looking out over the ocean, being close to ropes and smelling old musty mildew odors. I can't say how long I was on this ship. I just remember being on it for a very long ride.

Inside my head, or mind, the scene then changed somehow. I was asked by some type of force if I wanted to go into the future. It wasn't like a person or spirit. I never saw anyone or anything. I was just asked, and I was instantly inside a vehicle with a round window that I was peering out of. I saw a city that I thought was thousands of years into the future. There were very tall buildings and flying machines that looked like they came right out of a science fiction movie. It was a very complicated skyline and the city had a haze floating about halfway up around its structures. I was amazed at what I was seeing. It was nothing like I had ever experienced.

Then, without any communication, the scene changed again and I was in hell. I wasn't told where I was by anyone or anything, I just knew that it was hell, or possibly my personalized mental creation of it. It had giant machinery with huge red, blue, orange and multicolored rotating gears and the noise was deafening. The landscape of machines went on forever in all directions. There was an entity there, but I didn't interface with him; I just knew of his presence. Although I never saw it, this entity was very troublesome and scary. I knew that under no circumstance should I communicate with it.

The scenery changed again and I found myself standing on a large grassy hill. I was extremely powerful. My body appeared to be chiseled from a big block of wood. It was as if I was carved out of this huge block by a sculptor using a chainsaw. My arms and legs were muscled and cut like a bodybuilder on steroids. I must have been thirty to forty feet tall. I had no fear of anything!

Now, you might think that this was just another psychedelic overdose where the kid took a bit too much and had some sort of bad trip. Maybe it was. However, something strange occurred as I saw myself on that hill as a very powerful being. I must add that this trip was like nothing I had ever experienced. It made such an impression that I never touched any drugs after this. The experience was so real and so vivid that I can literally relive it forty-seven years later!

As I was standing there, all-powerful and all-knowing, I looked at my hands with outstretched arms. I then began a countdown using my fingers.

With all ten digits pointing outward, I heard myself say in a thunderous tone, "Ten." Then I folded my thumb inward on my left hand and said, "Nine." Then the index finger of my left hand, "Eight." A booming number—one minus the other, followed by each digit that I retracted. This was not a quick process. It was not in slow motion, but each number corresponding to the retracted digit took several seconds.

The countdown continued, "Three . . . Two . . ." When I got to "One," I saw my single forefinger on my right hand become profoundly huge, then it receded from my vision. That's when I shouted out at the top of my lungs, **"I'm God!"**

The entire scene turned black. I opened my eyes and found myself lying on my bed, naked, in front of all my guests that were staring at me. Awkward! I felt like they were looked at a mummy in a museum. The two very odd things about this event were, one, that after my countdown when I opened my eyes to see everyone gawking at my naked body, I was utterly and totally sober—sane as a judge, so to speak. It was as if I had never eaten any shrooms at all. I was lucid and knew exactly what had transpired with me. The second anomaly that's puzzled me ever since was the countdown itself.

Remember that I was out of it! I was on a grassy hill, looking like a giant animated chiseled block of wood, yet I was actually lying on my bed with about twenty-five people, guys and gals, looking at my junk. So, here it is . . .

How is it that I could have been aware ahead of time, when I started the slow and deliberate countdown, that when I got to "One," I would be instantly and totally snapped out of that mental environment where I believed that I was "God" on a grassy hill? Being God on a grassy hill was interesting enough, but how could I have known that, several minutes in the future, I would instantly become myself, totally sober and totally aware of my surrounding? The countdown must have had a purpose; or else ending with the number "one" would not have had any significance to my coming out of my mystic environment to one of total sobriety. The fact that the countdown started in one state of mind with the number ten and ended abruptly in another when I got to "one" had to have some correlation. Was I in some mental state where time did not exist and I could see the outcome of returning to my bodily consciousness several minutes before I got to the number one? Today, with a new understanding of time in a non-physical mental state, I can appreciate the mechanism of **how** I knew ahead of time where I would be when I arrived at the number one!

Here's how far out of my physical existence I was. What everyone there told me what I did during the time I was somewhere else had no resemblance to what I had experienced inside my consciousness. In my mental environment, I was in the far past, on an old sailing ship out at sea. I went into the future, staring out a flying machine's window looking out over a fantastic city. I went to hell and saw huge machinery. I stood on a hill as a giant chainsaw-sculpted moving wooden guy that counted down my return to Earth. What my guests and my wife told me what I did with my body was rip off all its clothes and began wandering outside in the front yard and wanted to go traipsing down the street. I began moving items from here to there in my living room and was babbling in some language no one understood. It's as if I were two completely individual me's.

Drugs can put us into another realm of existence. Psychedelics and prescription drugs can cause hallucinations and natural substances like peyote that Native Americans partake of can provide spiritual experiences. One particular spiritual experience that's become popular in the past decade is going to an ayahuasca retreat in South America. This drug is said to gush out a transcendent, life-altering experience. The end run is that one returns enlightened, calm, loose and open. The ayahuasca tourism industry has exploded in Peru, drawing people from all over the world. The only in-depth study of long-term ayahuasca users conducted found that its subjects have seen a reduction of drug addiction, reduction in depression and fewer anxiety disorders. What differentiates ayahuasca from Timothy Leary's "Turn on, tune in, drop out" movement is that it produces a willingness to remain in the mainstream of society. People found that it helps them to find something that resonates with their deeper values.

Many people that do an ayahuasca ceremony say that they actually communicate with a higher intelligence. A voice speaks with them and answers questions. Answers come back personal and pertinent to the one asking. Like in a near-death experience, a person is sometimes able to have a life review. A quote from the documentary, *The Nature of Things, with David Suzuki*: "Most people report revisiting the most significant events of their lives, like sequences in a chaotic film. The drinker is vaulted from one subconscious vision to the next, and his buried memories rise to the surface, it often leads to acute emotional catharsis."

Another drug that can induce an experience that resembles a near-death experience is ketamine. This drug blocks receptors in the brain for the neurotransmitter glutamate. The claim is that all features of a near-death experience can be produced by intravenous administration of 50 to 100 mg of ketamine. This includes traveling through a dark tunnel into a light, telepathic communication with God and visions of out-of-body experiences.

The fact that a drug can induce the characteristics of a near-death experience does not mean that people that have the near-death experience without drugs do not experience consciousness outside their bodies. The fact that veridical near-death experiences occur places drug-induced near-death experiences into a separate category. Therefore, we can conclude that near-death experiences fall into three categories. These are firstly those that tell about their near-death-like experience as a consequence of taking some drug. Secondly a near-death experience where those tell of their visions of tunnels, a life review and other things they saw. The third, and for me, the most important of all, is a veridical near-death experience, or veridical consciousness. This is where a person that flat-lines is fully aware and sees everything that's going on from a vantage remote from their physical body. They can also experience someone doing something in a separate room that they could not have seen and recounts the incident in a way that can be verified, hence the term, veridical.

The argument over whether there's life after death is not moot. From cases and experiences that defy the laws of space and time to knowledge obtained while the brain is in an altered state, to experiences verified by others, we must conclude that there's more to reality than what a conscious brain perceives from our purely physical realm.

CHAPTER 7

THE MAN IN THE PLAID SHIRT

"Do you think your dad had anything to do with my margarita tasting like Canadian Club?"

MY DAD OFTEN WORE A PLAID SHIRT, LIKE A HUNTING shirt, red squares separated with black stripes. When we lived in that little house in Ohio, a man would come and stand in the doorway of my bedroom and simply look at me in the middle of the night. I was terrified. He always had on a red plaid shirt like my dad wore, but since I knew my dad was asleep with my mom in their bedroom, I didn't associate this man with him.

This man was the same size as my dad, with black hair like my dad and never made any attempt to go any farther than the doorway. He came several times over a period of a couple of years, and then never returned. I often yelled out for my mom to come. She thought I was having a nightmare, but I was always fully awake when I saw him. He was as solid as the doorframe in which he was standing. When my mom arrived and turned on the light, he disappeared. What could this apparition have been?

One theory that I have come to accept is that this was actually my dad in some esoteric form. My reasoning for this is based on what I know about the conditions on the other side and the characteristics of time itself. You see, on the other side, time does not exist. In a later chapter I point out some physics of space-time in our universe that are so bizarre that it's nearly impossible to get your head around; however, these laws of physics are viable based on the mathematics of physics. But first, let me begin by simply saying that it is possible for a non-physical entity to move forward and backward in time. One must also understand that this "movement" is not performed in any physical manner, but rather with no other means than that of thought. In this instance, thought becomes a vehicle. Until I explain this in more detail with the support of quantum physics, simply humor me and pretend that this might in fact be true, or at least plausible.

My dad passed away of a brain aneurysm in 1995. Although this happened at that time, and the man in the plaid shirt visited me in the mid-fifties, what I understand now about the spirit realm and quantum physics allows for this phenomenon to actually happen. It's often said that spirits haunting hotels and houses are trapped there for an eternity until they are released. I'm not convinced of this idea one way or another. What does make sense for me is an understanding that time on the other side has no meaning. An eternity for a conscious being that's not part of a time continuum may not realize they have the mobility to project, or think themselves to any other *environment* of time that they wish. What I have referenced to here applies to a material earthly place.

I use the term environment because on the other side, that's more what it is rather than a place. I believe that a person that's been abruptly transformed into a spirit form, has abruptly died, doesn't yet understand the mechanism of their mobility relative to physical time and space. This could explain the haunting of places that go on for tens, even hundreds of years after some terrible event has taken place there. The condition in which spirits, or persons that have passed over, find themselves is an environment rather than a material place that has time associated with it.

From the standpoint of a non-material place, a non-earthly environment, or an environment that's on the other side, the term "place" does not apply if there is no earthly physicality attached to it. People that have had a near-death experience describe rooms, pastures or meadows, large rooms with no walls or other terms that connote a physical place. From my studies, environments can present themselves as places, but with a distinct difference. This environment, although very real to the experiencer, is comprised of pure thought, in contrast to a physical place here that is composed of atoms and molecules.

In near-death experiences, spirit guides often show themselves as tall beings, or cloaked human forms, often with no faces and sometimes emitting only light from hoods covering their luminous heads, or any number of various forms. In cases of people having hellish experiences, they are sometimes greeted by grotesque figures and experience horrible situations like having their flesh torn off or demons putting slimy things into their eye sockets or any despicable horror one can conjure up. Other entities will present themselves in a form most appropriate for the person to relate to. For example, Christians will often see Jesus, while Buddhists will be greeted by the Buddha, or a Hindu person will meet Lord Yamaraj; Muslims will see entities that praise Allah and Native Americans will see the environment of the happy hunting grounds. The range of experiences goes on to fit all beliefs and mindsets.

Near-death experiences are universal. All nationalities, creeds and cultures and age groups experience NDE's. It's not a Christian phenomenon, nor is it limited to any set of parameters of beliefs. Atheists experience the same general montage as the religiously inclined. The gamut from good to horrible, from love to blackness and confusion, have all been experienced. It's statistically been documented that only 1% to 14% of near-death experiences are negative while the majority are positive.

In the case of seeing the man in the plaid shirt, it's my opinion that this was in fact my dad, but from an environment of the spirit realm where time has no meaning. Just as spirit guides show themselves to NDE'ers in a form they can relate to, I believe that my dad wished to visit with me and my brother at the time of his passing and came to a physical place that was most familiar and nostalgic to him.

My brother and I were living in California when he died at his home in Mississippi. He was 2,000 miles away and we were one of the most important parts of his life. He had never been to the houses we were living in at the time. I don't know for sure whether I'm right in my belief, but this is what comes to me when I think about this event back in Ohio because this was not the only time the same man in the plaid shirt made his entrance.

About a year after my dad's death, my wife Rosaline and I were visiting her sister in Seattle. Her sister was learning line dancing at one of the Elks Lodges and had invited us to join her and her husband. So off to the Elks Lodge we went to find out what this line dancing stuff was all about. On a side bar, Rosaline now knows over one thousand dances and dances almost every day of the week.

It was fun and we were having a great time. There was an upstairs loft-looking attic area where tables were set up for us to enjoy socializing and drinks. The rafters were open beam and it had a log cabin atmosphere where the rafters joined the floor laid on top of ceiling joists. The tables were adorned with flower arrangements in vases and battery-powered candles were the only lighting. It was quaint and romantic.

Rosaline wanted a margarita, so I went to the small bar to get one margarita and one rusty nail—one of my favorites. I returned to our table, gave Rosaline her margarita and she began to sip it. "That's not a margarita; that tastes like Canadian Club. This bartender screwed up. Can you take it back and get me a margarita?" I tasted it and sure enough, it was Canadian Club. I know this taste because that was my dad's favorite mixed drink before he switched to beer, lots of beer. I returned it to the bartender saying that this was Canadian Club and not a margarita. She dipped a straw into it, put it into her mouth and tasted it. "That's a margarita," she said adamantly. She shoved it back toward me and told me that there was nothing she could do to make it taste more like a margarita.

I took a quick sip to let her know that I was an experienced drinker and highly disagreed with her. To my shock, it was in fact a margarita! I was pretty confused and embarrassed at that point and awkwardly ambled back to our table and handed it back to Rosaline without saying anything. She picked up the glass and took a sip. "Now, that's much better," she said with a satisfied look on her face.

I said, "The bartender didn't make a new drink. That's the same drink I brought you before, and what's more, she didn't do anything to it either."

"No way!" she said, shaking her head side to side. "That's not the same drink," she blurted. I assured her that it was the same glass, the same contents, with no changes whatsoever.

About that time I saw someone out of the corner of my eye moving in the darkness of the loft off to my left. It was the man in the plaid shirt walking slowly near to where the rafters joined the floor. He stopped, looked my way, and then simply evaporated. Rosaline was facing me and didn't see him, but, the look on my face caused her to widen her eyes and she asked, "What are you looking at?" as she turned around to peer into the darkened portion of the loft. I told her that I thought I just saw my dad. That plaid shirt, the hair and his diminutive size was unmistakable. I think we both got goose bumps all over our bodies at that moment. I've even got some right now writing this.

Then the thought came to Rosaline, "Do you think your Dad had anything to do with my margarita tasting like Canadian Club?"

I said, "Maybe. But that's not the first time I've seen the man in the plaid shirt that looked like my dad."

CHAPTER 8

HAVING THREE OUT-OF-BODY EXPERIENCES

I mysteriously found myself out in the side yard looking at a spider web glistening with dewdrops from the early morning sun.

IT WAS 1976 AND I WAS TWENTY-NINE WHEN MY INSATIABLE interest in the question, "Why are we here?" had pulled me into studying astral projection. I had heard that people could get out of their bodies and go wandering around the neighborhood or visit their friends at their house after dawning on some enigmatic, non-physical form. I began reading books on the subject. *The Astral Body, Magic and the Qubalah, The Techniques of Astral Projection, Man Outside Himself* and many others. I began looking into "white magic." In my early twenties, I had studied the Bible intensely and taught it for several years and was a bit concerned with "black magic," so I stayed away from any evil or devil stuff. I wasn't really sure that we didn't create the devil based on religious beliefs, movies about evil, the dark side and images conjured up from *Dante's Inferno.*

I contend that if the devil exists like he's portrayed according to our modern beliefs, how come he's not also portrayed in the same fashion in all past cultures? It's an idea that the devil's looks had its origin in the Egyptian god, Bes. However, Bes was a friendly, protective god. People that have studied NDE's report that God, or "All That Is," "The Source" and other descriptions of intense love, is a common experience. However, the overwhelming consensus in NDE research is that Satan, as a being, does not exist. There is scant evidence of anyone that's had a near-death experience having encountered such a being. That doesn't mean it's never happened.

Nonetheless, I avoid the dark side of anything just in case I create something I may regret. I did, however, practice the ritual of the banishing pentagram for a few months. For me, this was more of a mental state where one believes in something to the point that it becomes real in their minds. Maybe I didn't do it for long enough to reap any benefits. I turned toward the idea that astral projection would provide answers as to what we are composed of in the spirit, or non-physical form. If we can get outside our bodies, then the reality of a God, heaven and the spirit realm must be real. This would lend credibility that there is in fact an afterlife. Relying on blind faith just didn't satisfy my pragmatic thinking.

There were many techniques that I tried, and I began to think that I must not have the genetic material, or a strong enough spiritual side of me for it to work. Then I read about "the little method." This is when you get in bed or in a comfortable chair, get up and trace out a path around your house and return. In that path, you perform detailed actions like looking intently at a light switch; don't touch it, or turn it on, just look intently at it. Smell it and get a sense of what it smells like. Don't lick it to try to get some taste or make any other contact. Then move on to another spot in your house. Make sure that the stops you make to examine objects aren't things that are going to be in a different place in the future. Move to a table, a lamp or your faucet in the kitchen. Make four or five stops, and then return to your bed or chair. Do this every day for thirty days. The next month, do it on one day, and then the following day, do it only in your imagination. Do this for another thirty days, alternating between actually going through your route and doing it only in your mind.

Keep doing this until you can't tell the difference between having done it with your body and having done it in your mind. When you can't discern the difference, and you know that you are doing it in your mind, then, change your course. If you change your course and experience something new, while doing it in your mind, you have actually done it outside your body. You have attained the reality of astral projection.

I did this for several months, but was never able to change the course. I have no idea why this method didn't work for me.

But! I believed that there was something in the essence and desire of really wanting to do something and that there was always help from somewhere. I believed that there was something other than just our physical existence. My desire to experience getting out of my body was strong. I wanted to experience this—badly!

Then, it happened. Early one morning I opened what I believed were my eyes only to see that the ceiling was only a few inches from my face. I was a bit puzzled at first and turned what I believed was my head toward my left to look at the closet door. To my total amazement, what I saw was the very top of the closet door and not the usual view of the doorknob level I was used to. Rather than accepting that I was floating above my body, I got really excited and I slammed back into my body, jerking it so abruptly that I woke up my wife. She was a bit startled, thinking that a burglar was in the house, or something bad had happened that caused me to shake the bed so violently.

Another very interesting anomaly of this experience was that I distinctly got a glimpse of myself lying in the bed. It's as if I had 360-degree vision, because I was looking both up and down at the same time, but with my focus being more in the upward direction at the ceiling.

This was proof for me that we do in fact have a spirit body that is conscious outside the brain. I was elated that this had finally happened. For the next several days I tried the little method, but to no avail. It just wasn't working for me.

A few weeks passed and I had literally given up with the little method. I remained satisfied that we are spirit beings disposed into a physical container. The next question was, why?

I remained awed at the experience and continued reading about astral projection, its mechanisms, auras and other aspects of our astral bodies. Then one morning, I mysteriously found myself out in the side yard looking at a spider web glistening with dewdrops from the early morning sun. At first I thought that I was dreaming. But my mobility was different from what a dream was like. The bushes that the spider web was attached to had leaves that were, well, how can I say this—greener than green. The dewdrops refracted the sunlight in little prisms that radiated the colors of the rainbow in each drop. These were much larger and had more colors in them than the normal rainbow-like refractive index of dewdrops. Even the spider web was refracting the light in a similar manner. I saw the spider dead-center of his web and he was beautiful, and I don't really like spiders at all.

I then looked around and saw cars driving down Wilcox Avenue, but the sound was not like I was accustomed to. I could hear every little pebble embedded in the asphalt that the tires were rolling over. The sound was somewhat muffled, but distinct. I could hear the air being displaced as the cars whizzed through it. Then, like before, I got really excited and, *blam!* There I was back in bed. I immediately went to the window to take a look at the bushes where I believed I had been wandering. Sure enough, there was the spider web, there was the glistening sunlight at the exact angle I had observed and all the dewdrops were in the exact same place as I had seen. But the leaves had gone back to a normal dull green and the dewdrops didn't have that brilliant diamond necklace appearance. They had returned to normal dewdrops.

This experience happened one more time, a few weeks later and never happened again. The second time, I "walked" around a bit in the side yard. I closely examined avocados hanging from the avocado tree and a cable coming down from a telephone pole. After doing this, I found myself simply existing in the side yard. I had no body that I could see. I didn't go slamming back into my body like the first time, but rather I just opened my eyes and was back in my bed. I immediately went to the window to observe the avocado hanging from the tree limb just to verify that I wasn't having a lucid dream. Maybe the reason it never happened after that was because I had gotten my answer and was totally convinced after three events of being out of my body that we don't die, but rather we transform into an evanescent or invisible form while also retaining all the consciousness of self.

Chapter 9

Limitations of Thought

The seat of conflict.

WHENEVER I HAVE AN IDEA OR THOUGHT ABOUT something, I like to read what Wikipedia says about it. "Wiki" is such a fantastic tool to use when researching almost anything. Another source I like is Dictionary.com. I looked up "linear thinking" and the definition in Dictionary.com was, "a process of thought following known cycles or step-by-step progression where a response to a step must be elicited before another step is taken." Isn't that the way we think anyway? I know what they are trying to say, but I can't think of more than one thing at a time in any regard. All thoughts are strung together like adding one bead at a time onto necklace.

If I think of the color red, I can't see yellow, blue or pink at the same time unless I think of some mosaic that displays these colors in some sort of pattern. Then these colors recompose as a single thought. If I picture a scene from a movie, or even imagine a fictional scene, I can't also view a bunch of other scenes or pictures unless I change my thought to a single new scene or picture. I've never heard of anyone having the ability to think of multiple thoughts at the exact same time. If you can do this, then, you're very different from me.

I believe that we are limited in our thinking process by way of the physical construction of our brains. It's clear in my mind that everything that I've learned while alive in my physical form came into my memory archive one thought and idea at a time. That doesn't mean that after thoughts get into our memory they aren't multiplexed into external behaviors. What I mean is that we use millions of bits of data in order to move our bodies in such a way that allows us to drive a car, or play sports. These are learned behaviors one thought at a time, but are added to previous skills we've learned, such as control of our legs when we began to walk. We also use new data, one thought at a time, to create beliefs or to modify old ones.

All of us have limits on the amount of time we have to live. If we were to learn everything there is to know that's ever been written, everything about glaciers, birds, bees, etc., it would take as many lifetimes as there are people on the planet (just a guess). What I mean by this is that all of us contain only the amount of knowledge that's able to get into our memory banks one thought at a time over the same amount of time that everyone else has. Therefore, in any given length of time, different people learn different things. The concept of which is obvious: The different things that we've learned form different opinions and beliefs, and those diverging differences often bring about, and result in, conflicting ideas, again, obviously because of different content. If we all learned exactly the same things at the same time, then all ten-year-olds, all twenty-year-olds, all fifty-year-olds and so on would agree because they would all have the same data sets and get along perfectly with no conflicting ideologies.

This doesn't happen, and therefore, nurseries with one-, two- and three-year-olds will squabble over what we would consider little things. As we get older, the squabbles turn into fights and as we gain more power, they turn into war. Not all people fight and wage war, but you get the idea.

I watch the news every night. That's just one of my routines, probably the result of linear thinking where I decided I was interested in world affairs. Since I've had this idea about the **reason** why people disagree, or for that matter, agree on things, for this chapter I've focused more on the underlying reasons for people having diametrically opposed or similar views. Also, when people do agree, I believe they only agree within the scope of each one's limited understanding of what the other person actually said or was thinking. In other words, we never get an exact picture of someone else's thoughts. We only get an approximation based on some verbal explanation of the other person's data set. That's because each data set is a little different to extremely different from ours, even though we are discussing the same thing.

What that means is that we probably never totally agree with anyone on anything. I sometimes ask people, how many universes are there? Most people will say one. People that watched Morgan Freeman's *Through the Wormhole* may say that there are multiple universes based on the concept postulated by Richard Feynman's sum over histories. This is the idea that the universe breaks off into another one at intervals of Planck time—the smallest measurable amount of time. On the other hand, if one believes that the only universe that exists is the one that's inside our heads, the only knowledge set we possess, then, with 7.4 billion people alive today, there are 7.4 billion universes. What's more staggering is that no two people have the same information stored in their memory banks. Even twins growing up in the same household experience a very different set of circumstances.

With so many different exposures to the physical environment, it's a wonder anyone agrees on anything, even on a coarse level! But we do. Martin Luther King, Jr. said, "I refuse to accept the view that mankind is so tragically bound to the starless midnight of racism and war that bright daybreak of peace and brotherhood can never become a reality . . . I believe that unarmed truth and unconditional love will have the final word." Many people say that they agree with him, but what did he actually mean? What is the interpretation? John F. Kennedy said, "Mankind must put an end to war before war puts an end to mankind." Yes, many can agree with this and this one is pretty clear. And, Mahatma Gandhi said, "Non-violence is the greatest force at the disposal of mankind. It is mightier than the mightiest weapon of destruction devised by the ingenuity of man." I don't know when he said this, but since he was assassinated in 1948, it might have been before the atomic bomb was dropped over Nagasaki, Japan on August 6, 1945.

To disagree with these statements might put that person on a level of evil in the eyes of those adamantly agreeing with these men. In the beliefs of some, anyone opposed to the noblest of ideas for mankind might be regarded as evil. Although I admire what these men of good intentions said, I disagree that we will ever attain such conditions on the planet. By perceiving physical existence from individual perspectives, our ideas and thoughts will always differ, even though we are apparently voicing similar ideas. This exposes why we see painful sides and beautiful sides of life differently. It also provides the precious gift of diversity and newness of experiences. We're like ducklings jumping from their nests only to hit and bounce off the ground to make their own way into the world. Hitting the ground from heights sometimes hundreds of times their size must hurt. Yet, they fearlessly jump, only to experience the precarious perils and potential rewards that are in store for them in an unknown future.

Some might disagree with Dr. King based on the ideas that they are better, smarter or subscribe to some other belief. The radical Muslim must surely disagree with JFK's words, believing that only a jihad at all cost will bring peace and favor from Allah. And military leaders may believe that the only way to win a conflict is with bigger and more powerful weapons than your enemy has. Who's right? Within our own personal universe, by way of our beliefs, we all are. This is because within our individual psyche, it's impossible to be wrong. We are always right until a new right overwrites the old one. Only then does the psyche admit that it was wrong. But, now it's right again.

What may be assumed from our history is that we come here on this planet to experience physical existence of which opposition is a major segment of that learning process. Violence is mostly the result of a small number of people that create the largest number of conflicts. And in some form or irony, the rest of us are faced with the decision as to whether we accept or reject the lesson of love from their actions.

Chapter 10

Saiey, a Spirit Entity from the Eighth Sphere

"…at the time of your physical death you can be reflected upon with the satisfaction that it was a job well done."

IN MY "QUAINT AND CURIOUS VOLUMES OF FORGOTTEN LORE" (my library of books on every subject from UFO's, the occult, Kirlian photography, astral projection, but mostly comprising physics) I had read that one could transfer consciousness to inanimate objects. It's not anything new. Panpsychism is the view that consciousness is a universal feature of all things and is one of the oldest philosophical theories. If panpsychism exists, then with a little practice, one should be able to experience objects using techniques of consciousness transfer as it was presented in the lore I was reading at the time. I won't go into detail about the technique but it was supposed to allow one to feel what it's like to be a crystal, or a mousetrap. What would it be like to become a cell phone or a Boeing 747? There were no cell phones when I was trying this technique in 1977, but we did have a really nice glass doorknob in our upstairs bedroom. Being curious about so many things, I thought this might be something interesting to try.

Today, I don't espouse to such an idea. I believe that one can imagine being an inanimate object and apply ideas and feelings of the mind as to what a thimble (ouch), or even water might be experiencing if it were conscious. But to actually transfer consciousness into an object now seems a bit out of the realm of possibility. However, in one of the books I had read, the author claimed this was possible, so, I thought, why not try it? After all, Luke Skywalker, and for that matter any Jedi, could do it.

Hence, the upstairs glass doorknob on one of our bedroom doors became the object of focus. For several days I used the technique described in the book in order to become a doorknob. Now that I look back, I can think of so many other things I would have rather been than a doorknob. But, it was pretty, clear glass and glistened nicely in the light.

The result was lackluster. As much as I wanted to become a doorknob, it just wasn't in my cards. My ex-wife Shirley, who I still remain friends with, had a very different outcome. I taught her the technique and every now and then she would try it on the same glass doorknob. Fortunately, although she never became a doorknob, the doorknob became a door for something quite unexpected.

I was at work when I got the message that my wife was urgently trying to get a hold of me while I was out of the office. After I got home, I took one look at her and said, "What happened today? You look white as a ghost." In fact, it was a sort of ghost she had an encounter with.

When I inquired more about why she was desperately trying to get a hold of me, she proceeded to tell me her crazy day's story. That morning she was in the bedroom practicing the technique of consciousness transfer to the doorknob when she began to feel very strange, like something was taking over her voice. She then started to mumble inaudible words. She had no idea what she was saying. At first she just thought it was some strange phenomenon of her mind, like her subconscious playing a trick on her. She began to get frightened when her mouth wouldn't stop talking. Now that wasn't like Shirley. She was not the most talkative girl and was actually a pretty good listener.

When the voice kept babbling on and on, she actually fainted onto the floor. Both our kids were there and saw this happen. They were also very frightened as to what had just happened to their mother. After several minutes she came about, picked herself up off the floor and was very dazed from the incident. When she tried calling me at work, I was doing a source inspection for my company. She couldn't get a hold of me. She was so concerned about what had happened to her that she called my cousin Pierre in Glendale to come right away that something had happened to her that she couldn't explain.

My cousin drove from Glendale to Bell to see what was happening. By the time he got there, she had calmed down enough to have assessed some of the situation, that it must have been her concentrating on the doorknob that triggered something to enter her mind and take over her speech. But, why were the words unrecognizable? What language was she speaking in, if any? And, why was it that she couldn't stop it when she wanted to?

We talked the evening away about her experience. In my inquisitive state, I wasn't about to let a thing like this pass by me without delving further into it. This could lead to an answer to something, and I didn't even know what the question could even have been at the time but it was something that my curiosity didn't want let go of. As terrified as she was, I assured her that this was not something bad, that it was most likely a contact from the spirit world and that she really needed to pursue it. But in the back of my mind there was this little voice saying, "That's your wife. What if this is some sort of demon and she's going to be possessed? What if we will need to have a priest come out and do an exorcism?" I've been told that I'm a pretty persuasive guy. In the end, I convinced her to try it again just to see if she could bring the voice back.

Jane Roberts wrote a book with her husband called *Seth Speaks*, which is one volume of a set of books called *The Seth Material*. In it Jane has a spirit entity speak through her, thereby revealing many things about the spirit world. We didn't know about Jane Roberts at the time, and knowing what I know now, I would have been much less guilty about telling her that this was a good thing to do. In the end, it turned out to be a very good thing and Shirley never had to rotate her head 360-degrees and spit out green pea soup.

I came home from work about a week after the first event and she asked me, "What kind of name is Saiey?" (pronounced like the word "sigh" and the letter "E"). I told her that it sounded like a Middle Eastern name. She put out her hand inviting me to shake hands with her and said, "Meet Saiey." I knew what she meant by this. She had tried to be a doorknob again and the voice came back. Sure enough, it was benevolent. Saiey told us that he was a spirit from the eighth sphere, wherever that is, or was. Together we recorded thirty-seven cassette tapes, which is about thirty-seven hours worth of taping over a two-year period.

I transcribed all the tapes together and wrote a book titled *Saiey, A Spirit Entity From The Eighth Sphere*. In the meantime, *Seth Speaks* had made a big hit and became a best seller. When I sent the manuscript to a publisher, their response was that it was too mundane. That it's been done before. What they wanted was a malevolent ghost story that wreaked havoc in our household, wrung one of our kid's necks or turned the milk in the fridge into squashed frogs. I told them that Saiey was a really nice guy, ghost or whatever, and that he was a great source of knowledge into the spirit world. They weren't interested in Casper, the friendly ghost, or even one with the knowledge of life, God and the universe. They wanted terror, someone's head on a platter, or just simple torture and death!

I've reread Saiey's book after my research into NDE's, and it's actually more relevant and makes more sense today than it did to me in the late-seventies. Saiey talks of time as having no relevance in the spirit realm. He called God "All That Is," a title that has been referred to by many NDE'ers. He asked me many times why I was so concerned about the afterlife and the spirit realm, that what I should be more concerned with and connected to is my physical life, because that's where I am now.

I want to provide a bit of background on Shirley and my thoughts on why I believe channeling is a viable connection with something higher than ourselves. I married Shirley when she was fifteen and I was twenty. That equates to a ninth-grade education. Not that she wasn't a smart girl at the time; she was. However, the depth of philosophical intuition, coherence or just the orderliness of the conversation with Saiey didn't fit the profile of the Shirley I knew in her "Shirley" state. They were two very different personalities with very different mindsets.

There are only three possibilities that I can attribute to the in-depth content of that unfortunately unpublished book. The first is that Saiey was in fact a spirit entity from what he referred to as the eighth sphere. The second is that Shirley was able to connect with some form of higher self, a place within the subconscious where knowledge of everything she has ever connected with was stored. The third, she was faking it and made everything up.

The first possibility is the most intriguing, as it certainly had insightful and compelling information. With the second possibility, there is a chance that she might have come across some of the concepts that Saiey posed at some time in her past. These included some very complex ideas of time, the creation of the universe, the greater self and the concept of God. Which, by the way, Saiey avoided the term "God," and always used "All That Is." For me, the third is simply out of the question. Shirley was not prone to bouts of fancy and there were too many things that I was positive she simply didn't know.

I believe that it was my influence on Shirley that caused her to have even a modicum of interest in things like astral projection, astronomy, how the human body works and physics. It might be my higher-than-normal IQ that's always driven me to stretch the envelope or dig a deeper hole for myself. Or maybe I'm one of those risk-driven personality types. Pushing her into making further contact with Saiey provided me with just a bit more knowledge about my appetite for discovering why we are here. More so, by rereading its contents, it has added another piece of the puzzle that allows me to paint a picture and provide an answer as to where my mom and dad are.

Either way, the two-year experience with Saiey, recording all those sessions and writing it all down, was an anomaly and a journey that I'm glad I got to experience. I tend to lean toward the idea that it was in fact some intelligent source she tapped into. My reason for this is that Shirley never wrote any books, or had much of an inkling toward intellectual discovery or long-term conversation. On the other hand, Jane Roberts was a writer and poet and would have had a motive, book publishing. Yet, in these communications with Saiey, I felt I was in contact with a real entity that actually didn't have all the answers, but maintained clarity of thought and always remained on subject. Having had tons of conversations with Shirley in her normal state, she would meander over an entire map of diverting content while in her Saiey state, it always, and I mean *always* remained on point. Just this feature alone is a consideration that Saiey was not a creation of Shirley's conscious mind. In other words, she didn't fake this.

Another point that is noteworthy is that Saiey didn't portray himself as a Mr. Know-it-all. He humbly stated that he was not one of the first non-physical entities, and that although he was aware of the creation of the physical universe, he also stated that, "There always seems to have been matter to me . . ." He went on to say, "I cannot speak as if I were the creator of things that exist . . ."

What he does say is that his first existence was a being on Lemuria, now the island of Madagascar. Saiey described Lemuria as being off the coast of what we now know as Africa. This was a bit fascinating for me because I know Shirley was not interested in, nor was she knowledgeable in, geography any more than the man in the moon. Connecting Lemuria with Madagascar was my first inkling that Saiey may in fact be legitimate. Saiey said that this was his place of origin as a partially physical being. As time progressed, Lemurians became more and more physical until they achieved a nearly total physical form. I was sure that Shirley had no knowledge of Lemuria or Madagascar, let alone that they are one and the same and that it's located off the eastern coast of Africa.

Another fascinating thing about this is the fact that Saiey mentions that some of us may have had our origin in some physical form while most of us are returning humans by way of reincarnation. I can only read between the lines on this, since Saiey only mentions that his recollections of the creation of the universe are limited. But one line alluding to the fact that Saiey was a late entity in the scheme of the universe is, "I cannot speak as if I were the creator of things that exist such as this, so I am limited in my answers for you. What you want to know is something that you must find from the creator himself or from those who have created the physical matter." He continues with, "You would have to go many, many entities from me, where their resources are such that they can, and have the ability to, create such worlds."

This was disappointing for me to read as this began to put doubt that Saiey was for real, since he didn't have all the answers. After my years of studying NDE's, I've learned that we aren't much different on the other side when it comes to knowledge. I learned that we are still "us" and, although we rejoin with our higher selves, and can even merge with the immense knowledge of everything, not all of us have the desire to do that. And, what many report from near-death experiences is that there is still work that is being done on the other side. That means that the universe, both physical and non-physical, is more of a process than a static existence where there is a ceiling of knowledge. This could be interpreted to mean that should such a ceiling of knowledge be reached, the spirit of All That Is raises its level. Or, that this ceiling is continually being raised by way of added experiences of all living things.

I loved the last line he used before he basically signed off, which was the last time Shirley ever channeled him.

"Harmony and balance within your universe, becoming a finely-tuned physical entity, requires balancing the physical, the mental and the spiritual part of yourself. This will lead you into such an enchanting experience that at the time of your physical death you can be reflected upon with the satisfaction that it was a job well done."

Mom at two years old

Mom as I remember her: smiling all the time

Dad happy to see the rain

Dad who looked a lot like Don Ameche

Mom and Dad dancing to my brother playing the guitar

Geauga Lake with Dad getting ready to pour the foundation

Grandpa's platypus tractor

Dad's shoe shop in Cartierville

House where Mom saved the twin

The foam core that
was beating against
the wall

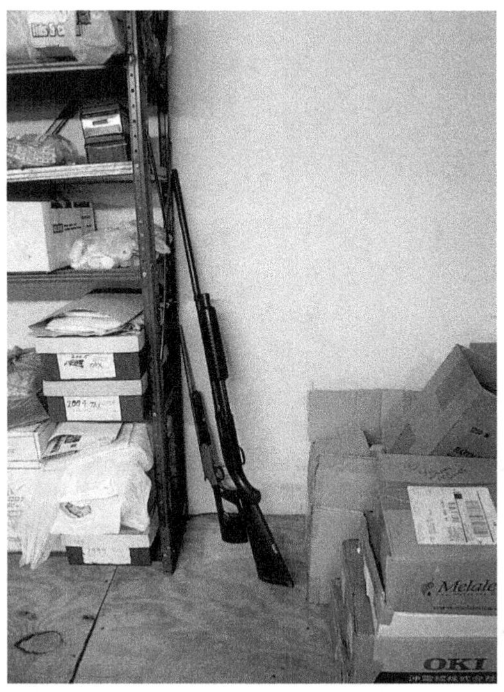

Dad's guns reconstructed propped up showing how they were before they fell forward

Dad's guns reconstructed showing them fallen over

The first ghost
photograph

The ghost going over a
desk

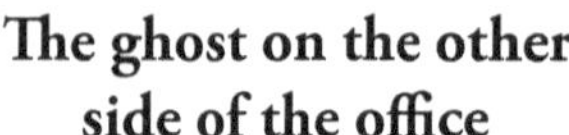

The ghost on the other
side of the office

UFO over our office in Torrance

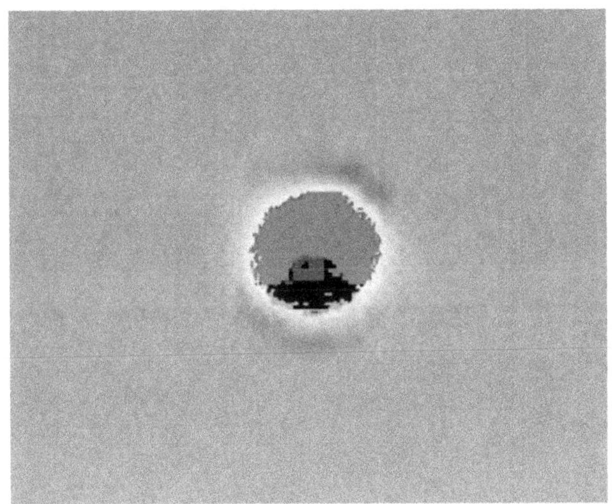

UFO image processed to indicate it was not
spherical

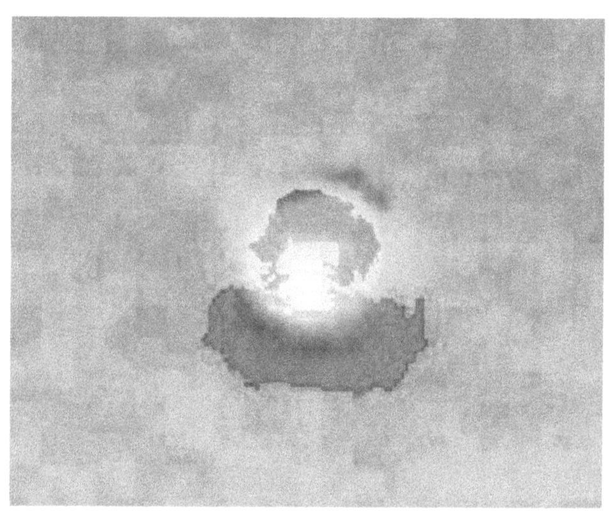

**UFO showing temperature change of air
ahead of it**

CHAPTER 11

MORE EVIDENCE OF SPIRIT VISITATIONS

In general, people don't see things they aren't looking for.

I DON'T KNOW IF I'M JUST LUCKY OR IF I FALL INTO THE ADAGE, "Be careful of what you wish for . . . you just might get it."

I will reiterate that I've always been interested in anything outside the mundane trappings of a normal life. "Curiosity killed the cat" is a proverb used to warn of the dangers of unnecessary investigation or experimentation. This may be true of people delving into ouija boards, or getting into black occultism and digging up something they wish they could reverse. In my case, I feel I've been a bit fortunate that it's most likely the mental vibes I may have been sending out, my subconscious desire to learn, discover or find evidence of the unusual that's presented itself for my edification. I'm bringing up a totally different subject for a very specific reason. Basically to enforce the fact that one finds what one looks for.

Since I've always had in interest in ghosts, UFO's and now an unquenchable thirst to discover if there's life after death, I tend to believe that thought can either reveal or produce evidence. I don't mean that if I think of seeing a UFO that one will magically appear in the sky or on my front lawn. What I feel is that if one believes in the possibility of UFO's, their eyes will be scanning the skies much more than someone that poo-poos the idea. Therefore, the person that says UFO's don't exist has much less chance of ever seeing one than the person that believes in them, notices something in the sky in their peripheral vision and takes the time to examine what it might be.

Dulling cognitive skills from the possibility that something exists reinforces the idea that they, in this case UFO's, don't exist. Since they don't believe in them, they'll never see one, and since they've never seen one, then they must not exist. To the non-believer, everything that flies is an airplane or a bird. For the believer, it's a plane, a bird, or possibly a UFO. Now that can be a bit misleading for the believer that believes in only these three options. In reality, there are many things in the sky, especially with all the things orbiting our planet that we've shot up there. The Goddard Space Flight Center lists over 2,700 satellites in orbit and over 25,000 pieces of debris up there.

The list of other things we can see in the sky is vast. There are not only planes and birds, but also meteors, comets, satellites, odd cloud formations, Venus, drones, military experiments, balloons of all sorts, Chinese lanterns, parachutists, the aurora, and if you're lucky, a supernova. And many of these can qualify as a UFO if you don't know what it is, since UFO merely stands for Unidentified Flying Object. Occasionally an object that's round and fairly flat, flying very slowly, sometimes glowing and photographed with a good high-definition camera shows up on the internet. That's *not* a UFO; that's what I would say is an IFO, an Identified Flying Object. What annoys me is when someone pitches the lid of a garbage can into the air and the photographer claims it was flying slowly and he saw big-headed guys flying it. Some claim their video was of an object flying too slow to be a conventional aircraft, but the frame rate was simply slowed to produce nothing more than a slow flying Frisbee. The easiest to spot are the computer graphics generated ones. In my mental universe, it's inconceivable for me to understand why someone would lie or fabricate this kind of deceit when there is so much evidence that many UFO's are real.

Without crediting myself as being overly pragmatic, many of the UFO's I've seen on YouTube are obvious fakes. That's for anyone reading this that have never seen a real UFO and don't believe in them and don't believe we have been, or are being visited by, another civilization in space. For those like me that have seen a real craft that doesn't fit the characteristics of any man-made flying machine, congratulations! If you are open to the possibility that we have or are being visited, but have never seen one, at least you are open-minded enough to allow new and unexpected information into your personal universe.

Yes, I've scanned the skies ever since I was a young boy after a double-inverted pie plate-looking craft flew over my house in Ohio. It was travelling about two to three miles per hour, walking speed. It looked at first like it was glowing a phosphorescent blue-green, but getting a better look at it as it went directly overhead, it looked more like a corona discharge where it was ionizing the air around it. It's like it was a big high-energy capacitor making what looked like an aura of soft lightening around its shell, merely giving the appearance that it was glowing.

My brother was in the same bedroom with me at the time. A loud humming sound woke me up. I opened my eyes and saw shadows moving against the house next door. The trees were casting these shadows from some moving light. I had to jump on my brother's bed so I could stare out the window at the craft that had slowly moved directly over our house. He got really mad and tried to throw me off his bed so he could go back to sleep. He doesn't even regret not looking out the window because he's just not interested in such things.

Here's an example in support of the idea that thought, or a belief in something creates evidence. In Rosaline's mind, meteors didn't exist simply because she had never seen one and quite frankly had little interest in astronomy or anything in the sky before she met me. I told her that the Leonid meteor shower was going to be the best one ever this year. This was on November 19, 2001. She was a bit curious but not excited, since it was going to be in the middle of the night and she loves her sleep. She went along with my suggestion that we drive out to Palmdale, rent a motel, wake up at 2:30 am and drive to some dark place in the desert and see what happens. To both our total amazement, and I've seen many meteors, we counted over a thousand meteors in the one hour before our necks began to lock into some permanent deformity. Some were coming in three and four in a row with huge debris trails behind them. Today, when driving at night, she gazes out the window and sees them on a regular basis.

Rosaline had never seen a UFO. After listening to my interest in such things, her attention to things in the sky had greatly expanded. On April 15, 2000 around 3:30 pm, she and her son Ricky were driving down Lomita Boulevard in Torrance on the way to our office when she spotted a silvery object fairly low in the sky, coming toward them, but also climbing upward. She asked Ricky to watch it. When he first saw it, he described it as being silvery-white oval having blue-like haze coming off the rear and purple-like haze coming off the front. When they arrived at the office, our door was locked, so Rosaline opened the mail slot and hollered, "Quick, get your camera, a UFO!"

I didn't hesitate. I grabbed my video camera and my telephoto lens, screwed it on, unlocked the door and ran out to the parking lot. When I got there, the object was almost directly overhead and had gone from oval to round. That means that it was not a balloon, because when Ricky saw it as an oval near the horizon and I saw it as round, that means it was more of a flattened shape, like a dinner plate. I laid down on the concrete, stuck my elbows in my ribs to steady my camera and got about eight seconds of video of the object.

I've included some shots of it where you can clearly see the blue and purple spike-like projections emanating from it. I did some histogram analysis on the object with some very interesting results which I have also included in the picture section.

What I'm getting at by pointing these incidents out is that there are things that people are oblivious to simply because they are not interested in them. And there are people that will stick to their beliefs, or disbelief, no matter how much evidence is placed under their noses. I believe there are many more anomalous events that happen on a regular basis than we can imagine.

To my knowledge, no statistical study has ever been done on the idea that UFO's exist or don't exist based on the number of people that believe in them and have seen one, versus the people that don't believe in them and have never seen one. That's most likely because very few credible people are interested in compromising their PhD or reputation on a study linked to the fringe kook population. However, there are some legitimate UFO researchers that are working hard to expose the fact that we have been visited by extraterrestrial beings.

I've heard the argument that extraterrestrials aren't visiting us because of the vast distances between stars. They say that it would take hundreds of years from nearby stars and thousands of years to get here from most of the stars we see in our nighttime sky even if they traveled at the speed of light.

What's not well known is that there is a method of propulsion being proposed that circumvents the limitation of light speed. Bob Lazar speaks of this in a video where travel is not linear, but rather the product of gravitational attraction. A craft with the technology to produce gravity could pull the fabric of space in toward them and instantly be in a location far ahead of them. Bob was actually indicted for revealing government "secrets." So, if what he said was made up, as many claim, why was he indicted? We don't indict people for simply making up stories in America. Lying while not under oath is not a punishable offense. Revealing government secrets after signing an agreement to keep your mouth shut is.

I'm listed as an author on the LIGO project, the Laser Interferometer Gravitational-Wave Observatory. When I worked on the project, I was informed that the purpose of LIGO was not merely to detect gravitational waves, as the recent discovery with so many Web articles claim. It was also to determine whether gravity propagates at some speed, namely the speed of light, or if gravity is an instantaneous force. To harness an instantaneous force would mean instant communication with astronauts on a Mars missions and instant military communication with any place on Earth. No more of that delay we hear on our long distance calls. But, more importantly, to harness gravity could result in instantaneous travel from point A to point B.

If aliens have in fact harnessed the force of gravity, it might account for us being visited by intelligent beings from very far away.

I recently received an email from someone that had a link with the heading, "detecting UFO's (if they exist) using LIGO and Co.?!" Since LIGO is a gravitational wave detector, what is the connection with it and UFO's? If UFO's use gravity to propel themselves, LIGO would be the perfect instrument to detect them. Here's the link: https://einstein.phys.uwm.edu/forum_thread.php?id=6771

The reason this link was sent to me is because of a very odd occurrence that happened to me. About sixteen years ago, I was in the bowels of the Caltech facility and recounted the incident to the link sender, who happened to be my son working as a design engineer in my office at the time. I had gone to see the space allotment for one of the telescopes I had designed for LIGO. When I was there I saw several military personnel. I wondered what military people were doing down there, since this was a National

Science Foundation project. I was with one of the project managers when, silly me, with my unobjective humor, blurted out, "I know what you guys are up to, you're making a UFO detector." The entire place went silent! I mean for about five minutes, no one said a peep! I was then taken to the far end of the huge room and told by the project manager, "We don't say things like that down here." So, in my little brain, I simply surmised that LIGO was a UFO detector *and* a laser interferometer.

Some notable people that believe(d) in UFO's include Richard Nixon, Ronald Reagan, John F. Kennedy, Mikhail Gorbachev, General Douglass MacArthur, Gordon Cooper, J. Edgar Hoover, Walter Cronkite, David Bowie, Elvis Presley, Dan Aykroyd and John Lennon, just to name a few. The Disclosure Project, an ambitious research project headed by Dr. Steven Greer including more than 500 government, military and intelligence people, disclosed personal, firsthand experience with UFO ET technology and the cover-up that keeps this information secret. Even with this overwhelming evidence, the only people that were convinced, or more convinced by the program, were the people that watched the show with interest because they believed in them in the first place. They were changed only to the degree that their beliefs were reinforced. Non-believers watched other TV shows like *Keeping Up with the Kardashians.*

When one is interested in a subject, for some reason, they pay attention and may even create an attraction for such events to occur. The idea that thoughts create reality is not a new concept. My pragmatic mind leans more toward the idea that interest in a subject creates cognitive awareness and therefore, experiences relating to that interest will be noticed rather than overlooked. Many books have been written about thoughts creating reality. In their context, these books mainly exemplify the idea that it's your thinking that directs your life. It's thought that can change your reality, and to me, this has always fallen into the category of obvious.

In the world of the occult, there are different aspects that thought can have on the physical, and for that matter, the non-physical. There are also physical ways to attract the non-physical. EVP (Electronic Voice Phenomena) has been used for many years and is becoming more widely accepted as a viable means to contact the dead. There are many techniques one can find on the Internet on how to attract spirit entities, or ghosts. It's also widely accepted that spirits are attracted to certain people more than others are. I may fall into this category.

After Rosaline's father passed away, I had many incidents of seeing a man wearing a fedora style hat in my left peripheral vision. For you younger ones, a fedora is one of those men's hats you see in the circa 1930's movies. Look up Dick Tracy. The man I saw was also wearing a dark overcoat. I could describe him in great detail, although I never saw him straight on; only out of the corner of my eye. When I described this man to Rosaline, she said that this is how she remembered her father dressing growing up in Taiwan. This was different from seeing the man in the plaid shirt, my dad, which I was able to see straight on. I would see him as if he was a real person standing to my left, but when I turned to look directly at him, he would disappear. The man with the fedora lasted for several weeks, mostly in the evenings after everyone had gone home, and then stopped. Some refer to these peripheral visions of people as shadow people.

Rosaline's father liked me and once walked over to me and gave me a big hug. Now you may think that there's not much to this, but, Rosaline is Chinese, and of course so was her father. I say this with conviction and evidence . . . Chinese men of the last generation just don't, or didn't hug! They might hug in today's new cultural environment, but the last generation was a manly man's world and hugging was for young girls. Even Chinese women of the past generation shunned hugging.

Maybe he had a desire to show himself after his passing because of his affection toward me, or the possibility that I'm just more prone to attracting entities from the other side, I don't really know. All I know is that I saw what I saw.

Another very interesting phenomenon that happened concerning Rosaline's side of the family was the time I was working on my computer in my office and I felt like something was going to happen. It was like I was looking through a heads-up display and was looking at some large object that was being thrown through a glass window, shattering not only the window, but also the entire window frame. I thought that we might experience an earthquake soon since I had predicted an earthquake one time before. Now, I'm *not* an earthquake predictor and my earthquake prediction may have just been a fluke.

This shattering window incident was about two days before Rosaline's mom suddenly passed away from a massive brain aneurysm. She was getting ready to go on stage to do her part in a senior citizen's play. Her head began to hurt and within minutes she was gone. I can't get the thought out of my mind that the sudden breaking of the window that I saw very clearly in my mind's eye was related with her sudden death.

Here's one that's out of character for me. Rosaline and I had flown to Las Vegas to do a little gambling. I'm not a gambler, since I know that the odds are against me. I will only play the slot machines, because it's fun and I know that I'm going to deplete my coins over some period of time. That day was a bit different. We had just arrived on a Friday afternoon. The first casino we went into, and the first one-arm-bandit I saw was a dollar machine. I *never* play the dollar machines. In fact, this was the very first and only dollar machine I ever put money into. For some reason, this machine was brighter than the others were. Not that it was lit with more lights; it just stood out as being brighter, more vivid. I took out a dollar, pulled on the handle and out popped $400! I cashed out, stuck the $400 in my pocket and didn't gamble the rest of the weekend. I wish I could do that all the time.

I have a theory that seeing into the future is more of a circumstantial function rather than something that can be turned on at will. It may be a playful act of one of your guides that has the ability to peer into a probability with perfect odds, or your guide is watching out for your wellbeing, as in the cases I've presented.

I had a very interesting experience occur in my office about fifteen years ago. One of my engineering associates came walking down my hallway. I could usually see a person coming down this hallway in full detail. This time what I saw was an unusually dark outline of a man walking but I couldn't see the normal details I was accustomed to. I had an uncomfortable feeling come over me as he came closer, even though I knew it was Jeff.

This was on a Thursday afternoon. Jeff committed suicide the next day. He told me that he stopped by just to say hi, but that was very much out of character for him. Jeff was a brilliant electronics engineer. I had worked with him for over five years. He had been having troubles with his wife and had talked with me about how I would handle his situation. A tremendous amount of guilt came over me after I heard of his death. I had listened to him and offered my advice, but had not reached out enough to help him overcome this trial in his life.

What was it that made him look so different to me as he walked down the hall? I can still see that image and it puzzles me to this day.

Another case of something that still haunts me is of a salesperson working with me on a project. He was a very skinny guy named Barry. Barry had a fantastic way with words. He could make me sound like I could walk on water with his embellishments. He never appeared to be ill in any way, just that he was really thin. One day I was talking to my brother on the phone and mentioned that I had a bad feeling that Barry was not going to be with us much longer. It was a passing statement, but had its roots in something I saw in Barry's skin that didn't look right the last time that I spoke with him.

I also saw a deep stare, not in the way he looked at me, but the inside of his pupils looked farther away than normal. I actually became a bit concerned and asked him if he was okay. I asked about his health directly and he said he was doing fine. He seemed a bit taken back by my question, but we changed the subject and went about our business. This was on a Wednesday, and that Friday he had a massive heart attack leaving a restaurant after having dinner with his girlfriend.

When I told my brother about Barry passing away, he said, "Boy, you called that one!"

We had a very close friend that was murdered in 2001 just before Christmas. Now, I didn't predict this and it was a real shock for us to get the news. When we got the call that she was dead, I got a very strange sensation that I knew details of what had happened. I told Rosaline that Reniece (name was changed to protect her identity), a person that was part of a multi-level marketing organization Rosaline was involved with at the time, knew something very important about the killing, but I couldn't make the connection. I kept telling Rosaline that Reniece knows all about this, but doesn't want to talk about it.

I must have given the impression that it was Reniece that did it, but that just didn't make sense. Then Rosaline told me that Reniece had a son that was a very scary guy. She said that he dealt in drugs. As soon as she said this, it was absolutely clear to me that he was the murderer. Rosaline asked me if she had been raped and I told her no. I then got the impression that Reniece's son hated Christine for some reason, but that's not the only reason he killed her. I distinctly got the impression that his motive, along with the fact that he hated Christine, was for money.

Christine was leaving the next morning for Taiwan to visit her parents for Christmas. Reniece's son got wind of this and believed since she was leaving for vacation that she would have cash on her or in her home. There was no evidence of break-in, so he must have knocked on her door, she opened it and he let himself in. She was murdered by having a telephone cord wrapped around her neck and strangled.

None of this was available when I mentioned that I believed Reniece's son was the murderer. None of the information about the murder was available when I told Rosaline that she was not raped. However, as the detectives did their discoveries, all of what I had felt and said was true. When the Torrance detective on the case questioned us, what I told him didn't appear to surprise him. He told us that Reniece's son was a pretty cold character. The evidence that put him away was Christine's DNA under his fingernails.

Was it Christine herself that may have wanted someone to know what had happened? I don't know this.

And last but not least . . .

My office is in our 12,000 square-foot building where I do engineering services, product design and development. I take people's ideas and turn them into products. I've been doing this for thirty-five years. This building moans, groans and creaks with thermal changes. There's always some sort of noise coming from the rafters, the walls and sometimes the floor. So, a ghost in this building seemed out of the question from ever being heard haunting around trying to scare someone. Also, I work very late into the evening and the noises are so common, I never associated them with spirits. Plus, I'm just not afraid of ghosts.

I had an employee named Rin that worked as office manager, purchasing agent and sometimes assembled some of our products. She was a very small girl from Thailand weighing 98 pounds, and I think that's right after she had lunch.

One afternoon she was in her office and I was in my separate office when we heard more than the usual building noises. She came creeping into my office when she heard the noise. This was a *bang, bang, bang, bang* sound coming from an office at the far end of the building. I got up out of my chair to investigate. Rin followed me to the far side of the building to the office where the noise was coming from. As we got closer to the back office, she got frightened and grabbed my arm, hiding behind me in case it might be a robber that I would get shot first. When we entered the back office, the banging continued. That's when her nails nearly penetrated the skin of my upper arm.

What was making the banging sound was a large piece of foam core (like a thick piece of illustration cardboard) that was between the wall and a bookcase. This piece was about three feet by four feet and a quarter-inch thick. It was banging violently, hitting the back of the bookcase and the wall, back and forth, back and forth. We watched this for about ten to fifteen seconds; then it stopped. I must mention that there are no open windows, no open doors, no wind or any sort of air movement in that room. It's completely closed off from any air disturbance whatsoever! We looked at each other with very wide-open eyes. I made a grimace, like, *WTF was that?* We know what we saw, but what in all blazes could have made that foam core beat against the wall and the bookcase so violently?

About a week went by and the same thing happened again. Again, Rin dug her nails into my flesh as she followed me into the back office. She said she followed me because she didn't want to be left alone in her office, that hiding behind me felt safer. I watched the foam core board beat against the wall again for ten to fifteen seconds and stop.

To this day I cannot explain how a piece of foam core board could have ever done what it was doing.

It was another week after that that we heard banging again from the same office. This time it sounded different. Again, the nails dug their way into my flesh. This time the foam core board was not moving, but the banging was coming from the ceiling above. It was coming from a book-case that was on the second floor of the back office.

We went out into the warehouse and went about halfway up the stairs to the mezzanine where the banging was coming from. There we saw another bookcase, heavy with items on its shelves, and it was banging vio-lently against the wall. Rin stopped following me as I went to the top of the stairs. She turned around and went back down to the warehouse floor.

I continued up to the mezzanine and when I got about halfway to the bookcase, it stopped moving.

I examined the bookcase and there was nothing unusual about it. Again, there is no air movement, no doors, nothing that could account for a bookcase to move like it did. However, there was one big finding that may account for the disturbance. The answer to the banging bookcase was not so much what I found, but why the banging occurred in the first place.

To me, the only connection I could make was when I saw two of my dad's guns, a 12-gauge shotgun and a .410 shotgun that were both lying flat on the floor. What's strange and unexplainable is that both these guns had been leaning in the corner of the bookcase and the wall before this incident. Something had caused them to pull away from being propped against this corner to fall forward and land flat on the floor. Was it my dad trying to get into contact with me? That's enough to make a believer out of the staunchest disbeliever in the supernatural, psychokinesis or just plain spooks.

Not to sound like a late-night infomercial, but that's not all! Another event was documented and photographed by my employee John. This happened in the same back office where the flailing foam core boards were seen. We had turned this room into a testing lab for the microscopes we were manufacturing. One late afternoon we got a visit from a real live ghost and I have included its photos in this book!

My grandson was working here at the time along with a machinist. I was out of the office during the incident and wish I had seen the apparition. Fortunately, the photos show what they witnessed.

What was told to me was that John went into the lab to do some testing when he saw what looked like a piece of fog hovering over a desk that was positioned against a corner. He thought something had caught fire and what he was seeing was smoke. As he got closer to the smoke, he noticed that there was no odor, so he knew a fire didn't cause it. The cloud remained there for several seconds and John called out to my grandson Alex and our machinist Phil to come take a look at this odd hovering cloud.

When they entered the office, the cloud began to move toward John. That's when he had the wherewithal to snatch his iPhone from his pocket and begin snapping photos of this moving piece of fog. He snapped off six photos of it climbing over a table and back down toward the center of the room, then over to a hutch where photos of my mom and dad, and Rosaline's mom and dad were placed on a glass shelf. Then it simply dissipated.

I keep these photos of the floating fog in a subdirectory in my computer under the title, Ghost of CC Design.

CHAPTER 12

FROM GOD TO ATHEIST BACK TO GOD

God was a little guy, small enough to fit in a box that somehow got put into Brother Andre's heart so he could heal people.

FOR ABOUT THIRTY-FIVE YEARS I VACILLATED BETWEEN being an atheist and an agnostic. When my mom passed, I had become, for the most part, an atheist even after getting out of my body and many other odd experiences. I believe that people need to reinforce their thoughts in things like paranormal events, UFO sightings or anything out of the realm of the explainable. I know I need to remind myself that these crazy things actually happened. And even then, after some time has passed, I shake my head side to side and have to attempt to reason out what caused certain things to happen that have no logical explanation. I often have to remind myself of these bizarre events and then ask myself the question, "Did that really happen?"

As I mentioned in the first chapter, I was born in 1947, in Montreal, Canada and Mom and Dad were a typical Roman Catholic, French Canadian couple raising their kids in the Catholic faith. I have many memories of those grand cathedrals in Montreal. One in particular is of visits to L'Oratoire Saint-Joseph. Or, in English, St Joseph's Oratory of Mount Royal, where thousands of miracles were professed to have taken place. The elaborate church was the vision of a sickly orphaned child named Alfred Bessette, often referred to as the Miracle Man, and later to become Brother

Andre who had a special devotion to Joseph, in the Bible, the father of Jesus.

Brother Andre was a small, unassuming man, ironically the son of a carpenter. He worked as a farmhand, a shoemaker, a baker and gave free haircuts to the students of Notre Dame College where he worked as super-intendent. It was here that some of his earliest miracles were preformed and witnessed by students and staff. His adoration of St. Joseph and a constant view of Mount Royal (Real in French) gave way to a vision of a church devoted to the Saint.

On October 15, 1904, construction of a small church began on Mount Royal. Soon after its construction, the church needed to be expanded because of the news spreading far and wide of Brother Andre's special gift of healing. Consequently, an addition to the church was constructed in 1924 at the highest point in Montreal. Hence, the basilica named L'Oratoire Saint-Joseph was begun. Brother Andre never saw the roof or its magnif-icent dome, and died January 6, 1937. Under construction for the next twenty-nine years, with its completion in 1966, it attracts more than two million visitors per year.

I was seven years old when I first visited the Oratory, which simply means a place of worship. We had taken a vacation from Ohio to visit aunts, uncles and cousins. I remember being excited about going there. As we got close to the huge front doors, I felt I was entering a very special place. I had been in many large churches before, so the main altar, the high ceiling and its grandiose dome made little impression on me. It was when I noticed lots of what looked like debris and garbage off to my left that an eerie feeling came over me. There, in the main hall, my eyes affixed on the hundreds of canes, wheel chairs, metal and wooden artificial legs and arm braces of all kinds that were hung onto or leaning against this promulgat-ing wall of the huge church. The items went from floor to ceiling. There appeared to be thousands of them.

At first I didn't know what all these things were doing in a church, but I quickly made sense that there was something special here, more special than I could have ever imagined. My Uncle Luke and Aunt Eva were with us, and my uncle explained that people were cured of all sorts of diseases here and these items were left behind as a testimonial to the many miracles that Brother Andre had performed as what he called "favors" to the afflicted. I was immersed in a state of bewilderment and awe. I was surely in the house where God lived, because who else but God could cause, through Brother Andre, all these people to be cured of so many diseases, crippling disabilities, and hardships. This was where bizarre miracles had taken place, and the gruesome appearance of all the old apparatuses designed to straighten legs, assist poorly operating arms, eyeglasses by the hundreds, mismatching shoes, and rusty braces of all sorts sent an uneasy shiver throughout my little body. It was not the miracles, but the thought of the wretched state of the bodies of those prior to these miracles that affected me the most.

But, there was an even more amazing object to behold that notable afternoon. It was enshrined in a large gold and velvet adorned structure off to the right side of the basilica's main hall. Inside this sacred-appearing structure was another smaller, open-sided, and very ornate box with something that must have been very important in there because there were many people waiting their turn to peer inside. "Was it God?" I thought. Could this be the place of all-importance, the source of miracles and healing? What was in there that was so interesting to all the people waiting so long to have a gaze at?

My mom and dad, my uncle and aunt and my brother all got in line to have our turn at what this could possibly be. They seemed to know what it was, but weren't telling me. As we got closer, the mysterious object began to have a form and a shape. It wasn't glowing like I thought God should. It was not making any music like angels singing. In fact, it wasn't doing anything at all. It was finally our turn to get a close look the mysterious thing of such great interest. I got up on my tiptoes to finally satisfy my curiosity and after looking at it for some time without being able to distinguish what it actually was, I had to be told that it was a human heart! It was the heart of Brother Andre. It was as if it was just hanging there in mid-air supported by nothing. The sides of the glass box housing the heart that the heart was in were covered with a red see-through cellophane to give it a living blood-red color. I stared at it for what seemed an eternity—probably nearly two minutes. This must be where God lived, inside Brother Andre's heart, since it was so elaborately decorated and so many people surrounded it, staring, whispering things to each other.

The heart of Brother Andre was preserved at the request of Archbishop Charbonneau of Montreal. This practice is traced back to early France, where the hearts of their kings were put on display as a sign of adoration.

Even as a child, the Oratory put me in a religious, maybe better, a spiritual frame of mind. No one spoke loudly and everyone looked interested and serious. There were black-robed priests walking around, and a few nuns here and there. I hadn't quite made the connection between Brother Andre and God, but I felt close to God that was inside that heart.

I was not the only one to be so impressed with the heart. On March 19th, 1973, thieves broke into the Oratory during the night and stole it. The great healer's heart was being held for a ransom of $50,000. The church refused to pay anything to get it back. They must have figured that it was of no value to anyone recognizing what it was, and they obviously could not put it on display for a fee to view. So, on December 21, 1974, it was quietly returned.

We returned from our vacation back to Ohio where I had a completely new perspective of God. God was a little guy, small enough to fit in a box that somehow got put into Brother Andre's heart so he could heal people. As I got older, this perspective and my perspective of little children's thinking processes broadened. Children are really creative. As I write of this event, it provides me with a deeper degree of understanding how beautifully simple children's minds work to make sense of the world around them. Kids, you gotta love 'em.

When I was between the ages of eight and ten years old, we went to church every Sunday. On the altar sat a golden container with a round base where the priest would pull out little things that were hard for me to see. That container is called the Tabernacle. I began to wonder if *this* was the place they kept God in when he was in Ohio. If so, what about the little box at St. Joseph's Oratory? Can God be in two places at once? I just lived in that question as I watched as the priest did his thing.

I would watch closely what the priest was doing, trying to make sense of it all. The priest would somehow produce little round pieces of bread and everyone would go to the altar to eat one. To me, they were having a little chunk of God for breakfast, but the priest always got the biggest piece and downed it with a glass of wine. I knew what wine was from my parents drinking it all the time. Since it seemed to make my parents feel good, it must make the priest feel good too. As I grew older, the mystery of what was going on faded into the practicality that those hosts were just pieces of bread and that the priest had to keep the wine somewhere. The whole church thing began to lose its veil of mystery.

After we moved to Arizona, then to California, we began to attend church less and less, and I got hip to the idea that God didn't live in a Catholic church, or any other church, let alone inside a little box. Going to church was relegated to midnight mass at Christmastime, and after my brother and I left home, I don't think my parents ever went again. However, the image of all those items hanging on the walls of the Oratory has always remained fresh in my mind. He must have performed miracles, but how?

Seeing Brother Andre's heart no longer impressed me as much as the evidence of miracles I witnessed at the Oratory. The fact that miracles must have happened is what may have set me on a path of spiritual belief that God was a really nice guy. So when I was invited to the Mormon Church, the Church of Jesus Christ of Latter-day Saints, I accepted that any church was good without hesitation since God loved everybody and Jesus was his little boy. Anyone believing in God was okay with me. I was fifteen years old when I began going to this church. The people were very nice to me. I liked their gatherings on Wednesday night. These were for teenagers and we sang, played games and learned about John Smith, but nothing about him having a bunch of wives. I looked them up on Wikipedia, and these girls weren't beauty contest material . . . Sarah Marietta Kingsley may have passed for a 6, but the others barely made it to 3. Yes, love must be blind.

My association with the Mormons was fairly short-lived. We moved to Mississippi, I had my bout with Huck in Jackson then we moved to the country, Flora, Mississippi. There I was invited to join the Baptist church. It was fun too. In my mind, all churches were good and were filled with good people. I really never learned much about God in these churches but singing hymns, listening to the preachers talk about Jesus and why you should give them money seemed very normal.

After I had my two kids and stopped doing any drugs altogether, a couple of very nice ladies knocked on my door. I was twenty-two years old and had, as I wrote about in earlier chapters, decided that my life was more important than hanging around with a bunch of long-haired hippies. Also, I hadn't learned anything about the meaning of life from them other than that one shroom experience that left me with more questions than answers. Maybe these two ladies actually were onto something, searching themselves, who knows? These two ladies (their names have been requested to be withheld) were from the Kingdom Hall of Jehovah's Witnesses and were so convincing about having found the truth about God that I went full bore into the study of the Bible, according to the beliefs of the Watchtower Society.

I have to give Jehovah's Witnesses credit for walking their talk. No Christmas, no birthdays, no Fourth of July, no St. Valentine's Day, no Father's or Mother's Day, not even your first-born child's potty-trained day! The only thing they celebrate is Jesus' last supper on Nisan 14, the first new moon of the spring equinox, which is the same day as the Jewish Passover. I must admit that I learned more about the Bible with Jehovah's Witnesses than I ever did with the Catholics, the Mormons and the Baptists put together. I might add that you will also learn more about the car you drive by joining a group of car fanatics that all drive the same car you do. To their credit, as a group, they really gave it their best shot at living by their beliefs, but even then, there was still hanky-panky within their walls.

So, after several years of intense Bible study, I became disillusioned by the entire religion thing, the whole idea of a God became absurd. Religious people lie, cheat and steal just like everyone else. In fact, I was more impressed with some of the people I met who were businessmen that displayed simple and honest integrity. That's not to say that businessmen have more integrity than religious people.

I often said if religion were totally replaced by integrity, we would live in a much better world. Another aspect of lack of integrity is the politician that will say anything for your vote, and then do as he pleases for four years, or a lifetime if he's a senator or something. When I saw so many religious leaders fall from grace, so to speak (Jimmy Swaggart, Jim Bakker, Ted Haggard, Kent Hovind, Robert Tilton, Billy James Hargis, Peter Popoff, Gilbert Deya, and on and on) I said to myself, "I'm outta here—this religion stuff just isn't for me."

For thirty-five years or so, I held onto the notion that you're born, you live and then you die—the end. There's no existence, no thought, no pain, no complaining, but then again, no Big Macs, no really good movies to watch, no sex, no Lamborghinis or that heavenly Bugatti Veyron—nothing.

I may have drifted side to side sometimes, wondering if there was a god, but mostly stayed my course. When you're dead, you're dead. In that mindset, I experienced the dichotomy of believing in ghosts, the supernatural, **and** that there was no god! I would convince myself that the idea of a god just can't be, because of all the bad things that happen on this planet. There are murders, children born with debilitating defects, soldiers having arms and legs blown off, heart attacks, boils, acne, toothaches and athlete's foot. A loving, caring God just couldn't have created genital herpes or a serious case of hemorrhoids. What's more, how could a Baptist preacher actually want to beat up one of Jehovah's Witnesses for wanting to discuss Bible Scripture with him? Yes! This actually happened to me! This is another time I thought I was going to be beat to death. I think I was more scared of this Baptist preacher than I was of Huck Graham. Huck just wanted to show he was king of his hill; the Baptist preacher believed he had God backing him!

Then a serendipitous thing happened. My much-loved mom died from a stroke. How can I say that this was a serendipitous event? Isn't serendipity a fortunate happenstance or pleasant surprise? Well, it is, and I can only say this now. When it happened, I was extremely angry. I stayed angry for a very long time. In fact to this day, I have a bit of difficulty even looking at my mom's photos because it brings back both anger and the deep sorrow I had of losing her. On the other hand, her passing has allowed me to reenter a world of belief in a Supreme Being. That change of belief might have come with some help from the other side, or out of my curious nature. Either way, Mom is not in that nonexistent state that I believed in for thirty-five years. The reason I've turned around is very simple. It hinges totally on my study of **veridical** near-death experiences and a reevaluation of my experiences with having gotten out of my body.

You may be thinking that if I did in fact get out of my body, then why would I become an atheist or even an agnostic? Why didn't this experience maintain a belief in a spirit realm and God in my logical-thinking brain, or at least a realization that we either are or have a spirit outside our bodies? Like I mentioned, I would sometimes drift into being open-minded to the idea that God exists, and then most of the time drift back out. I mostly just didn't think about it until some Jesus show came on TV. I always had an interest in Bible stuff after learning so much about it from years of study and viewing Brother Andre's heart inside that little box.

Veridical near-death experiences intrigued me because here was something tangible. Here was the hook I could hang my hat on. Veridical experiences didn't merely come from people that had a near-death experience and told of Jesus and angels carrying them off to play a harp on a soft, cottony cloud. These came from surgeons, paramedics, nurses, credible people that could verify an event of having been told by someone that was dead, who came back to tell that person what they (the surgeon, paramedic, nurse, etc.) were doing at the time the dead person was dead. For me, it couldn't get better than this.

When a dead person comes back and tells a nurse that she was the one that took the false teeth out of his mouth, that's veridical. These kinds of cases were all I intently studied for several months after my mom died. That's all I was interested in. I had a real hard time with the tunnel, visits from dead grandmas, tall beings that spoke through mental telepathy or talking trees. Yes, there was one person that said he communicated with barnyard animals and even the trees on his ranch. I have much more appreciation for these types of experiences now. Life, yes, all life matters! From humans, to animals, to plant life down to the microbial world, and yes, even inorganic matter is in union with All That Is!

CHAPTER 13

NEAR-DEATH EXPERIENCES AND RELGION

The growing interest in NDE's, increasing scientific studies of the phenomenon and exploitation of veridical evidence associated with them is sure to take root and grow within the matrix of faith-based religion.

WHAT ARE NEAR-DEATH EXPERIENCES? For most people reading this book, NDE's are quite familiar. For those not that familiar, they are defined as an event where a person experiences an impending death encompassing multiple possible sensations, including detachment from the body. These can also include leaving the body and levitating above their physical body and looking at themselves lying there. There can also be feelings of love, security, warmth, a presence of other entities, and a bright light often associated with being in the presence of God.

Near-death experiences are not new. Examples of NDE's appear in early Greek and Roman literature. One example is from Plutarch's *The Divine Vengeance*. Plutarch was a Greek historian born in 45 AD and died in 120 AD. He writes of a man from Soli, Cilicia, whose original name was Aridaeus, but was given a new name of Thispesius after his sojourn into the "other world." He had fallen and struck his head and died. He lay in his funeral bed for three days and then revived. During his death, "his intelligence was driven from his body," and "he had risen somewhat and was breathing with his whole being and seeing on all sides, his soul having opened wide as if it were a single eye." He noted the presence of souls in an elevated environment. A man he recognized as a child, but that had died greeted him. The man took Thispesius on a tour of various regions of the afterlife. Plutarch recounts that a "woman interposed, and he was suddenly pulled away as by a cord and cast in a strong and violent gust of wind upon his body, opened his eyes again almost from his very grave."

Many believe that this story is merely myth; however, a detailed study and comparison with modern near-death experiences conclude that the overall context may have been taken from experiences that could qualify as real.

Plato wrote about the Myth of Er, a story about a soldier that dies on the battlefield and awakens twelve days later on his funeral pyre, about to tell everyone about the soul's immortality and its progress after death. He returns to extol the virtues of wisdom, courage, love, justice and moderation.

Hieronymus Bosch paints a scene with souls ascending through a tunnel into a brilliant light that's strikingly similar to modern descriptions of going into a tunnel into a light brighter than the sun, but that doesn't hurt their eyes.

The oldest medical report occurred in 1740 by a physician named Pierre-Jean Monchaux. The case was of a patient in Paris who fell unconscious, then reported he saw a pure light, so pure and bright that he thought that he had gone to heaven. The same physician then compared that patient's experience with others that had recovered from drowning, hypothermia and hanging. At the time, the physician's explanation was that all these patients' vivid and strong sensations were the result of lack of blood flow to their brains.

This experience was compared with the "Greyson criteria" developed by professor and psychiatrist Dr. Bruce Greyson, used to establish a quantitative scale of NDE's. A score of 7 or higher out of a possible 32 classifies it as a near-death experience. It was determined that Dr. Jean-Pierre Monchaux's patient would have scored 12 out of these 32.

From the earliest of civilizations until today we have created ways in which death could be understood. We can view religion as a means to cope with the impending reality of death. Atheists view religion solely as a means to help people deal with the uncomfortable fact of our mortality. Agnostics fall into the middle trench, claiming they don't know and maybe don't want to know. Conversely, some religions espouse that there is a second birth, a spiritual existence where we live on for an eternity. And yet others believe that we recycle by way of reincarnation.

It's always been interesting for me to attend funerals where pastors, priests or family members eulogize the person who's in the box. In all the funeral ceremonies I've attended, I've never heard once mention that that person was in hell, suffering eternal punishment. They're invariably in a "better place." I would be interested in what they would say at a serial killer's funeral.

Religion, namely mainline Christian churches in America, suffered a decline during the 1960's and 1970's while some conservative denominations grew slowly. Graphs show church attendance dropped steadily from 1985 to 2000, made a resurgence from 2000 to 2004 and held steady up to 2012 before another resurgence from 2012 to 2014. Although church attendance has increased, this has to be compared to the Religious Landscape study of mainline Christians that in 2007, 73% were absolutely certain that God exists to only 66% in 2014. A Gallup poll showed that 96% believed in God in 1994 and 86% in 2014. This was the lowest figure since Gallup first asked the question in 1976.

What's happening in this information age based on insights gained from near-death experiences? The interest in what we're doing here as humans, why we're here and what the future of mankind holds will provide momentum for the promotion of near-death studies. Researchers John Audette, Bruce Greyson, Kenneth Ring and Michael Boborn founded IANDS, the International Association for Near-Death Studies in 1981. Today, IANDS has fifty locations and approximately 850 members with 14,628,500 hits to their website in 2011, according to their fact sheet. The number of hits shows that there is much interest in NDE's.

Interest has grown due to many veridical experiences that show evidence of anomalies that simply cannot be explained by science. There's a very interesting video on YouTube where a cardiac surgeon named Dr. Lloyd Rudy recounts an event about a man that survived after being pronounced dead. He says in an interview that after trying everything they could think of to keep this man alive, they finally had to give up. They buttoned the patient up so that an autopsy could be performed. The law requires that anyone that succumbs on the operating table must be autopsied. They had left some instruments running. Two of the machines, recording pulse, blood pressure and other vital signings, were left running their paper out onto the floor. Dr Lloyd and another surgeon left the operating room, removed their operating attire, and began discussing what they could have done to save this man. While they were talking, Dr. Rudy had his arms folded.

A crew entered the operating room to clean up. The doctors were out of the room for maybe twenty minutes when one of the clean-up crew called them back into the operating room. The monitoring machine began so show a slight blip of a heartbeat. They thought that this might be a normal activity that they sometimes see. When his heartbeat and breathing began to get stronger, Dr. Rudy shouted to get anesthesia back in the operating room. The man recovered with no neurological damage whatsoever even though he had no heartbeat for what they thought was twenty minutes!

When Dr. Rudy asked him what he experienced, if anything, he described the entire event from an elevated vantage point just as it had happened. One thing that was noteworthy for Dr. Rudy was that the patient had seen a cascade of Post-its stuck to a TV screen (computer monitor). Those were notes of calls Dr. Rudy had received during the operation that the nurse had stuck together, one over the top of the other, forming a long string. Another thing the patient described was Dr. Rudy standing with his arms folded outside the operating room. The patient could not have seen the Post-its when he was being wheeled into the operating room because they did not yet exist. He could not have seen Dr. Rudy with his arms folded because he was in a different room, dead! Dr. Rudy's video can be viewed at: https://www.youtube.com/watch?v=JL1oDuvQR08

At some time or another, I think most everyone looks for answers as to where we go after we die, especially after losing a loved one. There is a large-scale study called *The Aware Study* across Europe and America and another called *The Immortality Project* that have joined together to research this phenomenon.

We not only want to know what's going to happen after we die, but also want to know what the future of the world may bring. Many believe that our world is in chaos, that these times of turmoil need fixin'. In my view, and ask any historian, our times aren't really that much different from all the times of the past. As a populace, we tend to accentuate things that pertain to the immediate, that point in time we just happen to be in. After all, we can't do anything about the past and we have at best vague ideas what the future actually has in store. Futurists have some idea, but can only predict so far in advance based on their degree of knowledge as it relates to cycles, trends and human behaviors. James Dale Davidson and Lord William Rees-Mogg accurately predicted events with their 1994 book, *The Great Reckoning*. In retrospect, their timing was off by a couple of decades on the financial front, but the radical Islamic threat was, as the British say, "spot on."

Some of us believe that there are people that have special gifts allowing them to see into the future. Many NDE'ers claim to have that gift, or are in contact with the "Light" and ask about the future. What's interesting is that although some NDE'ers predict conditions or even events, most either fail, or the NDE'er didn't place an exact timeline to these predictions. I can only surmise that when asking about the future, it's easy to get the stream of time out of perspective. This is probably due to the fact that time relating to our physical world is so difficult to gauge in an environment where time has no meaning. Interestingly, Peter Fenwick's study of NDE's revealed that 24% of parents had premonitions about their children's death. According to odds ratio formulas, which are quite complex, this sample size percentage makes this number very significant.

Mellen-Thomas Benedict, one of the world's most famous near-death experiencers, says that our future is bright. This is in line with many NDE'ers. What he adds is that even though the future is foreseeable, since it comes from a place that essentially has no perception of time, these visions or information that's conveyed can be so far into the future that it's not really relevant to our times.

Benedict also says that we are living in one of the safest eras in history. He says that there has never been so much intelligence alive on the planet at any one time. Our lifestyles and the goods that have improved our quality of life are unprecedented. He also states that we're forming a new world, one that's coming that's nothing like what politicians are envisioning. It's not going to happen quickly though. We're looking at a couple of generations before real changes begin to occur, but even so, the future of mankind is not bleak. The petty differences we pass through are more personal than global. Large-scale shifts affecting us smaller entities occur slowly. Benedict says that the people running large corporations are not the bad guys. Contrary to common beliefs, these powerful people are actually very good people. The fact that large corporations employ millions of people is given bad treatment. But, in the future, our work will not be the prevalent point of our existence.

The middle class will reshape the future, and having a job will not be the center of living activity. The question for me is will I ever see this? Benedict says that the industrial revolution is over and the new world is one in which life will revolve around self-initiation. He also mentions that predictions are difficult to gauge. In the old days, if a prediction from a fortuneteller or astrologer was for a person with any power and it did not come about within a certain amount of time, they were killed. What we must take into consideration is that predictions that come from the non-physical must be looked at from the perspective of cosmic time. The change Benedict was shown is not pinpointed, but may be as much as 400 years out. In the meantime, we must contend with our immediate circumstances.

In one aspect of looking for answers, the question of whether there is life after death remains very popular. I've seen a tremendous increase in NDE videos in just the past five years. I've also seen non-profit and research organizations that have been created as a result of NDE data. I bring up the subject of near-death experiences with almost everyone I meet. In the past few years I've never run across anyone that hasn't heard of it. What's more, because I have a fairly extensive knowledge of the subject with respect to the average person that's not studied it, the conversation often merges right into it with people asking question after question. There is a deep level of interest from most people, especially from those that have recently lost a loved one.

As more people learn about it and as more people actually have a NDE, it's my belief that the coming world, and more so in America, will accept the phenomenon as factual. It's a belief of mine that this sort of information may somehow be incorporated into our religious faith as more religious leaders learn about these. We live in the information age. Knowledge is disseminated at light speed by way of the Internet. At no other time in history has information ever been so available. Videos on YouTube go *viral* and nearly anyone in the entire civilized world that has Internet, and most do, are able to view it. Religious leaders, even those that have less than noble values, may latch onto the idea of connections to a higher power through near-death studies to enhance their innate desire of prestige and, unfortunately, riches. I say unfortunately only because of the history of certain TV evangelists that fell off the turnip truck.

No one knows how long it will take before this phenomenon becomes inculcated into mainstream religion or accepted for what it's purported to be. The fact is that everyone I've talked to knows something about it, and it's something that religious and non-religious people tend to be more and more open to. It's the growing perception with the possibility that the NDE is real and offers a degree of comfort—that people can exit from their bodies and maintain some form of consciousness after death. This then leaves only a small mouse hole for the dissemination of a burning ever-after hell that's looking less plausible to the thinking person.

Dr. Bruce Greyson presented the idea that the brain is not where thought originates to the United Nations on September 11, 2008. His YouTube video can be seen at: https://www.youtube.com/watch?v=J_qBI-w7qyHU. His presentation was well received. It's only a matter of time before the evidence becomes overwhelming and the face of religion and society's concept of death is changed forever. This is because of the information age we've created by way of the Internet and portable computers, our cell phones. In the past, one had to read books, newspapers, and for the generation after World War II, it was the nightly television news that promulgated world events. Even during the seventies, eighties, and even into the first decade of the new millennium, the information age delivered limited data. Today, only sixteen years after the turn of this century one can find anything and everything, and with venues like Twitter, Facebook, YouTube, Pinterest and others, information can make it around the world in a very short amount of time. It's not like the Japanese soldier Hiroo Onada, who was on the Philippine island of Lubang and continued fighting the enemy for twenty-nine years after the end of the war.

On March 10, 1975, at the age of fifty-two, Onoda, in full uniform that was somehow still immaculately kept, marched out of the jungle and surrendered his samurai sword to the Philippine President Ferdinand Marcos. Marcos pardoned Onoda for his crimes, given that Onoda had thought he was still at war the entire time. If only he had a cell phone!

The growing interest in NDE's, increasing scientific studies of the phenomenon and exploitation of veridical evidence associated with them is sure to take root and grow within the matrix of faith-based religion. As these experiences continue to grow in number, and with as many people that have them, speaking openly about them without the fear of being ridiculed, or as in the past, institutionalized, we will begin to reshape antiquated religious dogma with new perspectives.

CHAPTER 14

MOM AND DAD DIED—THEY MUST BE SOMEWHERE

So the question, "Where are my mom and dad?" begins to clear up a bit—Aha! They've been uploaded!

WHEN IT COMES TO MY MOM, I CAN'T THINK OF ANYONE that didn't love her. All our friends called her "Mama Colombe." After my dad passed away in his sleep of a massive stroke, Mom moved to California to be close to her "two boys." My mom and I were very close and for some fortuitous human attraction, she loved Rosaline, my beautiful wife. They would play cards on Friday evenings, drink and swear, and have a wonderful time together. When my mom had a bad hand, she would say, "Shit." Rosaline said to her, "Mom! Don't say shit, shit's a bad word." To which my mom replied, "Shit's not a bad word, everybody does it." My mom appreciated Rosaline and her bubbly personality. Rosaline has this innate ability to turn a mundane gathering of people into an outright laughing party. She brings life into every room she occupies and my mom loved being in her company. They were more than friends; more than mother-in-law and daughter-in-law. It's like their souls were connected. They felt comfortable being with each other. I think Mom liked Rosaline visiting her than she did me.

Mom began bowling at age seventy-eight. When she started, there was a lady that literally hated her being on their bowling team because Mom was an old beginner. This lady wouldn't even talk to my mom when she asked for tips on how to improve her game. But, with every bowling experience, she improved. She got so good that during one tournament, she got a split on her first ball and strikes the rest of the entire game. This was a 290 at age eighty-five! She said that the entire bowling alley started noticing all those X's and came over to watch her throw that last ball. When she got a strike, she said the entire bowling alley went up in a roar. She said she felt like a queen for a day! But it didn't stop there. In another tournament, she did it again! I don't know if my mom ever ignored the lady that hated her when she started bowling after she became one of their most valuable team members. It wasn't in my mom's nature to treat anyone badly.

A friend of mine said that since this was recorded in a tournament, she should apply for the Guinness Book of World Records as the oldest person with the highest bowling score. I looked this up and it appears that no one remembers or even cares about anyone coming in second place with a mere 290. The only thing I could find were people that bowled perfect 300 scores, the oldest of which was a youngster of seventy-five named William June.

It wasn't uncommon to call Mom and she wasn't home. She loved to go out shopping, she bowled three to four times a week, took trips to Las Vegas and Laughlin, Nevada to gamble and an occasional cruise. She liked the penny and nickel machines because she could spend more time there before running out of her allotted gambling budget. Interestingly, that's exactly what I do.

Mom bowled her last game just a few days before she had a massive stroke in her home. A massive stroke was the same way that dad passed. She was very active right up to the end. It still pains me to see photographs of her smiling face. I don't have as uncomfortable of a feeling when I see my dad's pictures. I don't know why that is; maybe because I was seeing my mom so often after she moved to California. For several years as I looked at their pictures, I leaned more and more toward living in the question, where are my mom and dad? Where have they gone?

It's painful to lose a loved one. It may be a bit less painful to lose a parent that's had a good life and passes at a ripe old age. But, it's especially painful to lose a child, or someone in their prime that's a loved wife or husband. "Where did they go?" must surely be a common thought amongst those left behind. Where is my child? Where is my husband? Where is my wife? Where is my mom or my dad? Where do we go after we leave here, if anywhere?

If you've ever lost a loved one, you may have experienced eerie, uncanny or even paranormal feelings going through belongings they left behind. The smell of their belongings can last for months, even years, if they are kept that long. I had my mom's clothes and furniture in my warehouse for at least two years before I donated everything to surrounding neighbors. I can still recall the smell of her clothes, blankets and pillows. We had her body cremated for $750 by the Neptune Society. Not because it was low cost, but because she didn't want us to spend money for an elaborate, or even an average funeral. "You can just throw my body in the ocean, I won't need it," she would way. She had also often mentioned that if she were ever incapacitated on some life support machine, "for heaven's sake, pull the plug. If I can't bowl, I just want to go."

My dad donated his body to science. My mom told me that the first things they took out were his eyes. Now that may sound morbid, but NDE'ers reflect that when they saw their bodies, they had no attachment to it. They certainly didn't want to get back into it. Pam Reynolds said "it looked just like what it was, like in lack of life." I can imagine after being in a loving environment with lightness and freedom of mobility that getting back into a dead body might connote feelings of hesitation. But, that was Dad's choice, to have science make use of his old vehicle. He believed very much that "the good old Lord" would take care of him. That's what mattered to him most.

Since it wasn't unusual to call Mom and she would be out shopping or bowling, or talking on the phone with a friend, my brother didn't think there was anything to be alarmed about her not answering the phone, or that it was busy. After three days of trying to get a hold of her, my brother called me to ask if I had seen or talked to her. He said he'd been trying to call her and that her phone was always busy. He was used to calling her nearly every day to chat and catch up on her activities. He said he tried yesterday, the phone was busy all day, and it was again busy that day. Since he lived close to her and I was several miles away, I told him to get over there right away. I immediately knew that something was definitely wrong.

When he got there, the door was locked and her car was in the driveway. That wasn't right. He went around looking in the windows and got a glimpse of her in the living room. He immediately called 911 and they sent out the police and paramedics. The paramedics broke the door in and found her sitting in her favorite chair, smelling of urine. My brother said that the look on her face was unforgettable as he found her in that condition, in the living room, basically unable to move her body. She stared at him in relief that she had finally been found. Her eyes were large, wide open, but she couldn't speak. The telephone was on the floor lying next to her with the handset off the hook. I'm sure that she had been trying to make a call, but couldn't. It must have fallen on the floor as she attempted to call 911, or one of her boys. It was dreadful to think of her in that chair, sitting in her urine, helpless. She had been in the same chair for at least three days, maybe more. Just the thought still brings tears to my eyes. "Oh, no, that's my mom!" I said to myself.

She was taken to Torrance Memorial Hospital where she was given an IV and rehydrated. After about two hours, she began to whisper. I could barely hear her. She began blowing kisses at me letting me know that she loved me. All I could do was stare into her eyes. I was in a state where I didn't want to believe where I was or what I was doing. When Rosaline got there, Mom looked at her and gave her a thumbs-up sign that she was going to be back on her feet and bowling again soon. Shortly after this she looked at me and said in a barely audible voice, "I bowled 100 today." My heart sank. Something was terribly wrong. Firstly, she had not bowled that day and secondly, she was a far better bowler than to have bowled a 100. I kept that statement to myself because I was the only one that was close enough to hear it. For some reason I can only say was a gut instinct, I knew my mom was not walking out of that hospital, even though my brother insisted that she was going to be back home soon.

The doctors decided to wheel her away for a CAT scan of her brain because when they tried to give her water, she couldn't swallow, a sign of a severe stroke. After what looked promising to my brother, his wife Sonya, and Rosaline, but not for me, she had a massive seizure and began convulsing violently. It was a horrible sight for all of us. Rosaline and Sonya both went into tears. They loved Mom dearly. A nurse herded us out of her room as the doctor and two other nurses began working on her.

They were there for about twenty minutes. I could hear my mom writhing in pain and discomfort. I never want to hear that again from anyone, let alone someone that's so dearly loved. When we were in the hallway, the doctor came to us and explained that, after seeing the results of her brain scan, that she had been experiencing several mini-strokes for some time. This one was unrecoverable. We could put her on life support, but that she would not be responsive to any of us. Keeping with her wish to "pull the plug" if she couldn't bowl, we had to make the decision that still haunts us. Did we do the right thing? Could a miracle have brought Mom back?

She was placed in the hospital's hospice at our reluctant decision where she hung onto life for seven more days. We visited her every day. She was given morphine and another drug that calmed her seizures. It was so painful to see her have one. Her legs twitched day and night until the last couple of days where she lay tranquil with only the machine that monitored her breathing gave evidence that her body was still searching for one more breath. Mom had a tremendous will to live and was always a very strong woman. Maybe it was from mowing that acre of lawn every two weeks, or helping my dad build two houses, toting her bowling bag several days a week, or maybe from carrying all those beers to my dad. Up until the last time we saw her in good health, when we visited her she would begin to scurry about the kitchen asking what we wanted to drink, could she make something to eat for us, "I can make some spaghetti, or make some smoothies. What do you want?"

I have to be thankful for technology and the Internet for bringing me some solace about losing my mom and an understanding about "the good old Lord" taking care of my dad. I began an intense search for my mom and dad using this precious tool that my generation didn't have for most of our lives. Every day I looked for information on dying and life after death. In my mind, the question was why would a creator of life allow a beautiful person, inside and out, my mom, to not only die, but go out suffering in writhing pain from seizures that contorted her face and thrashed her body around like a rag doll?

For me, it's sometimes difficult to accept that I will die. It's much easier to have the thought that everyone else will. But, facing the fact that I'm going to die may not be so bad after all. That's exactly what one of our close friends said about his NDE. After having a heart attack outside a 7-Eleven, Dan found himself floating above his body looking at the paramedics working on him. He was revived on the way to the hospital. Upon inquiring about his NDE, his simple words were, "If that's dying, it ain't bad." Hearing it from a YouTube video is different from hearing it from someone you know very well.

Many NDE'rs say that we're isolated from certain knowledge of what happens after death. We will all transition from what we perceive as life into what we have been veiled from, and for a very good reason. Not knowing what's on the other side is at the crux of the mystery of life in this universe. It's what we, as living entities, aren't meant to know simply because if we did, we would run our lives much differently but we would be missing the perfect reason for being here in the first place. Not knowing this manifests itself in our behavior as humans. There are things we simply would never learn here if we knew all about the afterlife.

One of the first places I looked into where I could find my mom and my dad was inside Raymond Moody's book, *Life After Life*. Not that they were actually in there—like I would flip the pages and out they would pop—just kidding. This book was my early glimpse into the possibility that Mom and Dad were somewhere and not nowhere. I had read it back in the late seventies, but merely out of curiosity. Delving back into it opened a whole new expanse.

The transition in my belief in an afterlife started with a detailed review of Dr. Moody's *Life After Life*. Many people are familiar with this book, but it's worth reiterating a few of the examples of NDE's he wrote about. For those of you that have read the book, or are familiar with it and near-death experiences, you may wish to gloss through or even skip the rest of this chapter.

Dr. Moody tells the story of a young female migrant worker that had a near-death experience in a hospital and told her doctor and her nurse (she was actually a medically-trained social worker) about it. Her doctor explained the best he could that this was part of the brain chemistry shutting down and that it was just a dream-like experience associated with the anesthetic. When she tried to convince her nurse that her experience was more real than when she was in her conscious body, it's reported that she too reiterated the good doctor's explanation. The migrant worker said that she saw and heard everything going on around her body, that she left her body and to her amazement was able to fly up through the floors of the hospital and onto the roof. She described a blue tennis shoe with a scuff mark near the toe, that its lace was under the heel, and that it was on the ledge of one of the windows of the hospital. The girl's persistence in clinging to her story caused the nurse to take action. The nurse finally found the shoe on the third floor, on a window ledge that was on the north end of the building.

Another fact that's rarely mentioned about the social worker is that six years earlier she had had her own near-death experience. This may account for the reason the social worker took it upon herself to go and look for the tennis shoe. When the social worker went looking for the shoe, to her amazement, she found it exactly as the girl had described. This well-documented event was the beginning of several researchers' interest in the possibility that the age-old phenomenon of out-of-body experiences brought about by someone that has flat-lined may have some substance.

This is the case that started Dr. Moody's research into NDE's. Christopher Hitchens, an atheist critic of this case says in a trite public presentation that the names and places were never revealed. To set the story straight, it took place in April of 1976 at Harborview Medical Center in Seattle, Washington. The woman that found the shoe was, as mentioned, not a nurse, she was a medically-trained social worker named Kimberly Clark Sharp. The patient was Maria, and yes, it was a real event.

Dr. Moody's video, *Life After Life*, which can be viewed in its entirety on YouTube, tells the stories of six people that have had near-death experiences. At the time of my early research, I was open to any glimpse of the possibility that Mom and Dad could be found somewhere and that they just couldn't be nowhere. I hoped that I would find a place or existence where they might be floating on some great cloud with my dad playing his guitar, singing with Mom harmonizing or maybe Mom bringing Dad his anticipated cold glass of beer.

I was impressed with Dr. Moody's video interviews that focused on veridical experiences in contrast to experiences of people seeing Jesus, God, angels and other esoteric visions. His movie told the story of Dr. George Rodonaia's body spending three days in the morgue of a Russian hospital after being struck by a car driven by the KGB. While his body lay in the freezer of the morgue, he visited different parts of the hospital. When he saw a baby girl in the newborn ward that was continually crying, he understood her, communicated with her by thought and found that she had a "broken" (dislocated) hip. Moments before his autopsy, the coroner discovered that George was alive. In the recovery room, he told his doctor to inform the parents of the baby girl he had communicated with, that the problem was with her hip. As it turned out, the baby girl did in fact have a dislocated hip. After putting it back into place, she immediately stopped crying.

On December 1, 1943, Dr. George Ritchie was pronounced dead of lobar pneumonia while in a military hospital at Camp Bartley, Texas. But George was not aware that he had died; only that something was different. His desire was to make it to Richmond, Virginia to begin his medical classes. Not wanting to miss his opportunity, he began looking for his uniform. He experienced going down a hallway and passing right through a ward boy in charge of securing doors, making sure lights were off and so on. Still, he was determined to begin his medical classes in Richmond.

This determination was so intense that the next thing he experienced was flying at a tremendous speed toward Richmond. He had made it to Vicksburg, Mississippi to an all-night café where he could not communicate with anyone. No one could see or hear him. He didn't quite know what to make of it until he returned to the army hospital and saw a body that he recognized as his own. He finally realized and accepted the fact that he was dead at twenty years of age. He had a life review and was shown many aspects of the other side. Unexpectedly, nine minutes after being pronounced dead, he returned to life with no neurological damage. I recommend watching his video on YouTube. Eight months after the incident, he was driving through Vicksburg and recognized the all-night café that he had stopped at while out of his body. His book, *My Life After Dying*, is a detailed account of the various realms of the afterlife that he encountered.

A glimmer of hope that Mom and Dad could be somewhere rather than nowhere began to emerge. This hope enlarged itself with incident after incident from patients who had died on the operating table, or in accidents they were able to describe in great detail, events that they had no possible way of knowing unless they had in fact gotten out of their bodies. Ambulance paramedics told stories of flat-lined bodies they had picked up that later described the scene and events of difficulties such as inserting endotracheal tubes or the act of defibrillation. Cardiologists told of patients flat-lining after the surgical team had done everything they could, only to have the patient suddenly wake up all by themselves. One particular patient later told his surgeon exactly what he was discussing about the operation and what might have gone wrong, relating word for word what the surgeon had said and with whom he was having the conversation with. So, doctors out there, you need to keep the humor down after your patient has flat-lined or you may have an embarrassing encounter afterward.

Vicky Noratuk was blind from birth. She was involved in an auto accident and was brought into the emergency room for corrective surgery. While they were operating on her, she found herself outside her body in a near-death experience. From the ceiling of the operating room, she could see for the first time, and rather than it being a wonderful experience, it frightened her.

This fear of gaining sight coincides with people born blind and given sight later in life. An example of one patient who had his sight removed after having it surgically instated was horrified when describing seeing a car coming toward him even though he was on the sidewalk and the car was in the street where it should have been. In many of these cases, patients, rather than being overjoyed about being given the gift of sight, often preferred to have their sight removed due to fearful experiences such as these.

Then there is the incident of Pam Reynolds Lowery. Her experience comes closest to an experiment where one would be taken into death for the purpose of revival, just to find out what a person experiences when they are dead. She was diagnosed with a large tumor at the base of her skull. The procedure required to remove the aneurysm was highly risky with a low chance of success. However, without it, she was at risk of it bursting with tragic results. Many doctors declined to operate to remove it. Dr. Robert Spetzler decided to take on her case. They didn't want her to be aware during the surgery, as in some brain surgeries, nor did they want her to be asleep. Her procedure involved what is called hypothermic cardiac arrest, or a standstill operation. This involved cooling the body and stopping circulation. Blood is drained from the body to eliminate blood pressure. The patient is clinically dead during the entire operation.

Most patients can only tolerate thirty minutes of "standstill" without significant neurological dysfunction. When this is extended to longer than forty minutes, there is a marked increase in the incidence of brain injury.

Pam was put to sleep, her eyes taped shut and clicking devices were put in her ears to monitor the brain's activity and ensure that there was nothing going on. She remembered nothing of being taken into the operating room until she suddenly heard a very unpleasant whirring noise. She then "popped" out the top of her head and found herself looking at her body from a vantage overlooking the doctor as if she were sitting on his shoulder. Pam knew that this was her body, but didn't care about it.

The doctor had told her that they were going to use a bone saw to open her skull. Expecting to see a saw, what one would normally expect a saw to look like, what she observed was a tool that looked more like a drill or even more so, as Pam described it, her electric toothbrush. She also overheard one of the nurses say, "Doctor, we have a problem here," to which the doctor said, "Try the other side." When she looked toward what the nurse was talking about, she noticed they were looking down toward her upper thighs. That's when she wondered what they were doing down there; this was supposed to be brain surgery. The artery that was to be used to drain her blood was too small for the catheter. Fortunately the other leg's artery was large enough and the operation proceeded.

These and other incidents were related by Pam to the doctor after the operation. Dr. Spetzler states in the movie, *The Day I Died* by the BBC, that in her state, there is no possible way that anyone could see, hear or feel when in the state Pam was in.

What Pam further described in her near-death state was a light that she was drawn closer and closer to. She recognized her uncle and many other people who had passed away. She asked if God was the light, and her uncle said, "No, the light is when God breathes." Pam stated that the longer she was there, the more she liked it.

Her uncle told her that she needed to go back, but she didn't want to go back. She knew if she went back that she would be in pain, so her uncle gave her a "push," and then she found herself back in her body. Pam's husband saw her transform after the experience. She became much more idealistic and less judgmental. Pam got a highly developed sense of empathy. "She could be standing in line at a grocery store and detect people there who were troubled, some of them so much so that it could move her to tears." A fellow singer-songwriter commented, "After her near-death experience, she would call me from time to time to find out if something was bothering me. And, she would be right! In her phone conversations, she could describe the rooms of my house even though she had never been in it."

Amazingly, Pam was in "standstill" for over an hour and suffered no brain damage.

As more accounts of veridical experiences were found in my searches for evidence of life after death, the more convinced I became that we don't die and that my mom and dad were somewhere.

Near-death experiences must align themselves with out-of-body experiences. Out-of-body experiences exist, at least for me, because I had had three of them. Since this is true, we have to rethink the role of the brain as the seat of consciousness. It must be factually accepted that one can have sentience without the main component, the physical body and more so, the brain. We must rethink the idea that the brain is the structure where thinking originates, in direct opposition to what has scientifically and medically been taught for decades, even centuries.

If one can perceive, think and realize the self outside this container, then what is the carrier of the mind in such a state? In addition, if one does in fact believe in God, then one must also accept that consciousness can exist outside dielectric materialism. Without the belief that one can exist outside their body, then one can therefore believe that God need not exist.

What is the role of the brain if consciousness is possible without it? One can draw only one conclusion; that the brain acts as the gateway between our physical senses that form sensory perception and the non-physical entity we can hence label as our spirit, higher self, or mind. Therefore, for the upload into the mind, the brain processes our vision, sense of touch, taste, hearing, smell and all other perceptions of physical existence.

This upload has been suggested by a theory called Orchestrated Objective Reduction, which was developed by theoretical physicist Sir Roger Penrose and anesthesiologist Stuart Hameroff. Their research suggests that consciousness can be found inside the microtubules of the brain cells. At death, they suggest that the information energy inside these microtubules does not simply disappear, but follows the first law of thermodynamics, which says energy cannot be created nor destroyed but can only be converted. If this is true, then the energy of brain information must therefore be converted into something else. That "something else" may very well be pure conscious energy that comprises us as a spiritual being.

I've found no data or investigations as to whether this is a dynamic process that's continually being uploaded as we proceed through the arrow of time, or whether it's an upload due to some trauma such as believing one is about to die, or death itself.

Evidence that some people can experience out-of-body consciousness suggests that death is not necessary for this conversion, or upload, to occur. The requirement is merely that a certain condition takes place such as some experiential trauma, a drug-induced brain change or lack of oxygen to the brain that changes the energy state of the microtubules. This would account for many of the theories that discredit real NDE's and astral projection as the result of mere shutdown of the brain via the massive release of dimethyltryptamine, or that NDE's can be replicated using the drug ketamine or ayahuasca.

We can also draw the conclusion that since we can exist outside our bodies in spirit form, so can the spirit of God exist in a non-physical realm.

But, **where,** or more precisely, **what** is this realm, this plane of existence that resides so close to or possibly within us, juxtaposed beside or inside us, communicating somehow with our physical brains? Is it also possible that our universe resides somehow within God rather than God being external to it?

The evidence of NDE'ers being given a choice to proceed into the heavenly realm or return to their bodies poses an interesting hypothesis. There has never been an incident where a NDE'er has said, yes, I want to go forward into the next realm, actually gone into that plane and then, changed their mind and come back. This threshold is obviously some barrier that if crossed, there is no turning back. Therefore it can be concluded that all NDE'ers have in fact **not** gone to *heaven* but have merely gone to its gate to so speak. If that's the case, then, all of which NDE'ers have experienced must therefore be like an intermediate realm between the physical plane and the spirit realm of an actual heaven.

One can then draw the conclusion that there is a non-physical existence that can be accessed by way of astral projection, drug induced out-of-body experiences or some traumatic excitement of impending death and the near-death experience itself. From this realm there exists a voluntary return path or one is told that it's not their time and they must go back. Many authorities and Bible scholars publish their descriptions of what heaven is like, but mostly these renderings are faith-based. Beyond this, I believe we have little tangible information on the higher planes from which there is no return except by way of reincaration.

So the question, "Where are my mom and dad?" begins to clear up a bit—Aha! They've been uploaded!

CHAPTER 15

WHY WE ARE HERE

One WW2 soldier said that when he was in hand-to-hand combat and was forced to thrust his bayonet into the chest of his enemy, he no longer felt hate for that soldier.

NOW THAT MY RESEARCH HAD BEGUN TO REVEAL SOME sense as to where my mom and dad went, my curiosity shifted to why they, and for that matter, why we all exist in the first place. Why is anyone here? Why are the animals, plants and even microbes here? For that matter, why is the Universe here?

Roberta Grimes is a successful lawyer and an advocate of near-death studies. I have a hard time remembering names, probably because I'm a right-brain thinker. I'm really good at remembering shapes and mechanical contraptions, materials, plastic parts and things like that, but names of people, places and even names of things don't register as well as seeing objects inside my mind. Since Roberta has these really cute dimples, I called her Grandma Dimples around the office. Not that she's old; for heaven's sake, I'm a great grandpa. I have to add that I love watching Roberta's videos. Her enthusiasm and energy coupled with her logical thinking puts her on the cutting edge of research into life after death and spiritual matters.

Roberta had a spiritual encounter with a being of light when she was eight years old, in 1955. I just did the math and we're the same age. She had another visit by the light when she was twenty. She's written several books on the subject of life after death. She says that the physical realm is a necessary environment for exercising our potential to love. Her tenet for this is that in the spirit realm, love prevails, and if everyone in that realm exercises love, there is nothing to resist, or push against for that love to grow. She likens it to working out in a gym where there is resistance for muscles to grow and get stronger. In the spirit realm, there is no hiding of thoughts. All spirits communicate by some telepathic method therefore there's no misunderstanding.

Consequently, because there is no misunderstanding, nothing can be hidden or concealed. The lie does not exist in the higher planes, neither is there deceit, or avarice. This only exists on the lower vibrational states, but as Dr. George Ritchie's experience reveals, even on the lower planes, thoughts are transparent. On the higher vibrational planes, love prevails and all of the negative aspects of physical existence such as stealing, fighting, lying and so on simply cannot exist. That doesn't mean that there is no growth of knowledge or experiences from other entities, especially those coming from this physical realm that have crossed over with rich new tales to share. It does mean that in such a spiritually perfect environment, for love to be more fully experienced or even expanded, then it would make sense that if you can't go up any more, you can always lower the floor.

This can be appreciated using an example of eating your favorite food each and every day. After so many meals, you get used to it, and lowering your standard increases your appreciation of how great your favorite food actually is. Rather than filet mignon, we'll just have hot dogs for the next two months. In comparison to spiritual love, this may be a poor example. However, this is the concept. Roberta says that it's here in the physical that one can learn to love your enemy, or forgive others' transgressions against you. It's here that misunderstandings lead to escalating conflicts that go all the way up to all-out war where comparisons between good and evil can be experienced. Some soldiers have questioned what they're actually accomplishing by killing people, questioning for a moment why they're experiencing such atrocities.

One WW2 soldier said that when he was in hand-to-hand combat and was forced to thrust his bayonet into the chest of his enemy, he no longer felt hate for that soldier. It became for him a deep compassion, a strange feeling that came over him when he gazed into this enemy's eyes that was fighting for his life. The worldly ideology he was fighting for left him for that moment. On the other hand, what would have gone through the mind of his enemy performing the same act?

My research has pointed me in the direction that the overall realm of spirit existence is comprised of vibrational levels. What is actually vibrating in a non-physical existence is not clear. There also appears to be lower levels of existence where negativity has its lower vibrational effects. If we were to measure thought in terms of frequency, we could label higher frequencies as more pure, noble, altruistic, benevolent, and so on. Lower frequencies could be tagged as hate, anger, revenge, aggression, etc. This could imply that the mere act of creating, or having a thought type, puts you at a certain spiritual level. Maintaining a negative thought will suspend you on a lower vibrational level. Attaining and maintaining what we can refer to as positive thought, thoughts for noble intentions, love and learning for the purpose of spiritual growth will elevate one's level to a higher vibration and hence a higher level. The vibrational level of thought might even be that which actually creates such a level.

This is not to say that the afterlife is a place that has a physical structure like a multi-story building with floors vibrating at various frequencies, but certainly has a hierarchy that's rooted in thought type. It also has the mechanisms to produce form from thought, but only to a certain frequency level. There seems to be a limit to how high a frequency can go. This may be why some NDE'ers see flowers, fields and meadows since they are on lower, but not necessarily lowest levels and the longer they are there, they appear ascend to where they have more spiritual experiences. On the lower vibrational levels there are houses and anything else that one can create with the mind. As one ascends, so to speak, to higher levels, the landscape turns evanescent and thoughts create more feelings of a spiritual nature, culminating on the highest level into pure love.

In between, there are references to varying activities, such as people in learning mode seen in huge libraries, people engaged in various physical activities such as working in factories, people that appear to be in a deep hypnotic sleep waiting for the rapture, and on and on. The conclusion I've derived from these descriptions is that we bring our luggage, bags of shit to jewelry boxes with us. Everything except the kitchen sink has been described, and I'm not sure we don't bring that with us also. From people on lower levels doing horrible things to higher spiritual planes of love, the gamut of heavenly activities appears to be endless. A revealing aspect of love is described when souls entrapped in some deplorable state are not forgotten—that they are loved. A change of thought is all that is needed and they are quickly snatched from a negatively-charged environment into a new state consumed by love from whomever or whatever reached out to answer their plea.

Coming back down to our physical universe, I believe there are many worlds with intelligent life on them. It would be very interesting to experience what their creations in the lower vibrational levels might look like after their physical death. I would like to see what kinds of houses they build for themselves and what kinds of vehicles they create. This is speculative on my part.

So, why **are** we here?

The physical world we reside in offers many opportunities for experiencing happiness; however, we get caught up in the throes of our own desires. Many go after money as a means to satisfy a desire to be happy. Young adolescents are told they must have a college education in order to be successful, implying that this will bring happiness in the form of a good job and higher pay later on. Toymakers woo young children on television with enticing commercials while infomercials tout how much happier you will be if you send them three payments of $29.95 for something you've never seen before and never knew you needed. The reality of "having" is far removed from the emotion of "wanting." It's almost a universal motivation to want what we don't have based on what we see or hear about something presented in an enticing manner. It's also common to lose appreciation for something after we've had it for a while.

One particular line that comes to mind is from the old movie *Blazing Saddles*, where Madeline Kahn says, "It's not the money, it's the stuff." Materialism is a tendency to consider material possessions and physical comfort as more important than spiritual values. In philosophy, it's a monism that matter is the fundamental substance of nature, and that all phenomena, including consciousness, are identical to material connections. From my experience, this definition didn't originate with anyone that's popped out of their body to experience the intense love as expressed on the other side.

Materialism is an aspect of being here, alive with the freedom to play with our stuff. Could it be that it's this material form we're disposed into that invokes an innate desire to obtain "stuff"? I must admit that I'm guilty of loving stuff myself. I use the word "love" in the form of conceptual semantics, as in, "I love my car." I have a warehouse full of stuff and often think of the time when I will have to leave my stuff behind. I'm not obsessed with having stuff, and my attachment to stuff, especially certain items of a personal nature, simply brings me joy. It would bring me much sadness to have to part with it. Rosaline is a collector of stuff too. I tell her that she was born with packratitis disposaphobia. Her stuff is very different from mine. I love technical stuff like cameras, telescopes, microscopes, machines, computers and tools. She loves bags, colored paper, pens, knives, scissors, shoes, etc. etc. etc. I will say that if you can name it, it's in our warehouse! What is it about stuff that appears to make us happy?

The old television show *Lifestyles of the Rich and Famous* hosted by Robin Leach painted images of glamour, prestige and riches. But how do the rich and famous compare on a "happy" scale to poor people?

Here's a synopsis of a five-year study of some daily habits of rich people versus poor people.

- 82% of wealthy people were happy, while 98% of poor people were unhappy.

- 78% of wealthy people were happy with their marriage, while only 53% of poor people were happy.

- 93% of wealthy people were happy because they loved what they did for a living, while 85% of the poor were unhappy with what they did.

- And, of course, 0% of wealthy people were unhappy due to their financial condition, but 98% of poor people were unhappy.

There's a stipulation to these findings. The opposite side of having money is that not having it and either wanting it or needing it leads to an overall sense of unhappiness in the form of marital stress that can lead to health issues and can negatively impact the lives of other family members.

An Oxfam report came to the conclusion that wealth doesn't make the rich happier, but that the lack thereof makes the poor sadder. The study revealed that although the rich don't get a joy bump from their income, the poor do receive a sense of lack of control and lack of dignity in their lives.

In the Bible, which I often refer to as "Great works by Holly Bibble," it's not money that's the root of all evil, it's the love of money. The rich are not left standing without their own set of challenges. One of the greatest fears that a person has after a life of being poor and suddenly coming into money is losing it. Another is the fear of being hounded by friends and relatives for loans or people just asking for some of their money. Fear of lawsuits is another. Does my spouse really love me? Will my identity be stolen? Will my kids become spoiled brats with no perception of the value of money?

In the end, rich people admit an uncomfortable fact, that money solves most problems. It's a liberator and with enough of it, it offers peace of mind. As the singer Tallulah Bankhead once said, "I've been rich and I've been poor, and rich is better."

Many of the rich lead lives that are not much different than the middle class. And if an average cross section of the rich were gauged on an unhappy scale, we would not find a great disparity between rich people that are unhappy with their lives than those in the middle class or even the poor that are unhappy. To sum this up, when someone is unhappy, no amount of money or stuff will *make* them happy.

Tony Robbins, a rich motivational speaker, once stated that if a truly miserable poor person all of a sudden became rich, he would simply become rich and miserable.

So what about the super rich, what do the super rich really want? Although the super rich have enough money, there are still things that they psychologically lack. In a nutshell, the super rich aren't motivated by money, at least not after they've gotten their fill of it. They have enough for themselves and, in some cases, for many generations after them. A British study revealed that the rich are basically looking to be loved and honored. They work late into the night so that they can walk into a room full of strangers and be recognized by their deformed ego-driven personalities. They refer to the super rich as ambitious, narcissistically damaged and craven people in any society. The study refers to the founder of modern economics, Adam Smith, as identifying the "two chief motivating factors in life, the love of money and the love of glory." I disagree with Adam

Smith on one point, and that is that I believe that love of money and glory is *the super achiever's*, or *wannabe achiever's* chief motivation factor in life, and not a general statement that applies to everyone. There are enough people that would rather simply be comfortable, and this greatly deflates Adam Smith's notion.

In a similar way that the rich want recognition, a universal motivation for being happy is the desire to be loved. This is a basic need all humans have. This basic need comes in many colors, shapes and forms. In other words, the need is as complex as we are different from each other. These needs can entail romantic love, parental love, love from relatives, friends and even strangers. The Greek word "agape" refers to the highest form of love. It's also referred to as charitable love. In essence this love entails good will, benevolence and delight. It overarches the three others, storgē (pronounced store-gay), philia and eros.

Storgē is liking someone through the fondness of familiarity, family members or people who relate in familiar ways that have otherwise found themselves bonded by chance.

Philia is the love between friends as close as siblings in strength and duration. The friendship is the strong bond existing between people who share common values or activities. The city Philadelphia, the city of brotherly love, gets its name from this.

Eros is love in the sense of being in love, or loving someone in a romantic way. There is a distinction between lust and love; wanting a woman and wanting a particular woman. However in modern interpretation, eros is associated with erotic love.

It isn't surprising that most of us believe that a significant determinant of our happiness is whether we feel loved and cared for. The desire to love and care for others is hardwired because it's a two-way street between the giver and receiver. Small acts of kindness generate as much happiness as do lofty acts. A study was conducted with participants being given $5 and $20 as part of an experiment. Both groups were asked to spend the money on themselves or on others. It turned out that those who spent the money on others felt happier about their actions than those people that spent it on themselves did. Interestingly, it didn't make a difference whether it was the $5 or the $20; the degree of happiness derived was the same.

Violence, crime, torture and all the abominations of worldly existence have to be included in any attempt at figuring out why we're here. We not only need to know what makes us happy, but also what it is that stirs negative feelings that lead to hurtful actions. Exclusion of negative aspects of life would be like the ostrich's head being buried in the sand. Conflict is unavoidable and may be an important, integral and necessary part of the Grand Design of the universe. We live in a conflicting universe. The earth revolves around the sun. The conflicting forces, the centrifugal force of the earth wanting to fling itself out into space and the centripetal force of gravity from the sun keeping it in its orbit exemplify this. Every action produces a reaction, as illustrated in a poem I wrote in high school:

> I think there's nothing more relieving than a hearty sneeze.
> One so strong, so powerful, it can bend the tops of trees.
>
> At first there's a tickling of the nose, and then there is a notion.
> But then you fear and hesitate from Newton's law of motion.
>
> When climax comes your lungs are filled and then there's a
>   contraction.
> With pressure released, off you'll go from an opposite and equal
>   reaction.

This poem illustrates a conflict on a personal and imaginary scale, but any opposing force, view, and action is in fact a form of conflict.

The conflict between good and evil, conflicts arising within families over what show to watch, conflicting ideologies of how to govern countries, even conflicts of biological systems within our bodies comprise an all-inclusive concept that's part of the grand scale of organization in the universe.

This can be illustrated with a little humor. There was this ant that was talking to another about the state of affairs of the humans. They surmised that humans only had a few more generations before they would annihilate themselves, after which the ants would then rule the planet. To which the other one responded, "Red or black?"

No matter how peace in the world is vented with good intentions or mere rhetoric by world leaders, no matter how much it's wanted and desired, it's my personal belief, and your prerogative to disagree, that conflict is here to stay. Conflict has been around since the beginning of the universe. It has permeated civilizations, local tribal colonies, led to world wars and on to astronomical events such as supernovae. A synonym to conflict is also a collision. What makes anyone that has their thinking hat on straight believe that world peace is achievable when there has always been something going on that factions disagree about? This includes all the conflicting actions that have been occurring for billions of years in the natural events within the universe—from meteors entering the earth's atmosphere today to, yes, all the way back to the Big Bang.

Chris Hedges says in his book, *What Every Person Should Know About War*, "War is defined as an active conflict that has claimed more than 1,000 lives. Of the past 3,400 years humans have been entirely at peace for 268 of them, or just 8 percent of recorded history." What he doesn't mention are the minor conflicts that may have occurred during that 268 years where less than 1,000 people were killed. He doesn't say anything about conflicting ideologies present during the time of apparent peace. Today, Christianity is not at war with Islam; however, there are certain individuals that wish we were, and in the world of radical Islam, war against Western values has been declared. And, in that declaration, more than 1,000 people have been killed over a radical religious ideology.

In the context of this work, the thoughts provoked by the definition of conflict beg the question, what can we learn from it? Why does conflict play such a dominant role in our interplay with others? Or, what sort of world would it be without it? It would be naïve to assume such a world is possible. According to NDE'ers, it's our choice to enter into a physical form and experience life from the starting point of an erased past. Without the process of having all knowledge removed, how could there be growth within the confines of new possibilities? It's the contention of many NDE'ers that we know all our probable actions in our journey through life before we are born. That's not to say we are predestined. I discuss this concept more below about free will in light of probabilities. In support of Roberta Grimes's work, we come here in order to expand, or experience spiritual growth, and spiritual expansion cannot occur in a perfect realm.

To illustrate this point, one NDE'er stated that on the other side, the victim of a murder holds no animosity or any sort of emotional negativity toward his murderer. Views of these types are not part of the paradigm of the physical realm. And, on the other side, it's not even forgiveness as we perceive, but the fact that the actions pertaining to this worldly realm take on a different meaning. It's not like meeting someone that murdered you and saying, "Oh, hi there. You're the guy that murdered me, how are you doing today?" The non-physical, spiritual realm operates on a different baseline. Retaliation produces nothing of value because there is nothing to be gained in an environment of love. The experiences of living in this physical form can manifest themselves in crude and painful ways for the special purpose of expanding our spiritual self. We also have the choice to exercise love within the dirges of physical existence. Conflict reduces the power of love while giving, understanding, exercising compassion are additive constructs to love. Going back to the Source with a review filled with hate, conflict, animosity will only result in having to come back to try it again, or remaining on lower, abhorrent levels.

I personally accept the idea that, according to most NDE'ers, we all had an existence before we were born. We formulated a life's environment into which we have been immersed in order to experience things that cannot be experienced in the non-physical realm. We learn, expand and grow from the environment that we have set out for ourselves. We have seen all the probable outcomes of our life in this physical environment and live out a single path by way of choices, thus terminating the continuation of further probable outcomes. As an example, there may be several routes one can take to a friend's house. Before you leave the house, you imagine every possible route and can see in your mind's eye every turn, every stop sign, every tree on the side of the road of every street. These are all the probabilities that are part of the routes you have the choice to take. Then, you get into your car and as you take that first turn, you have eliminated all the remaining probable choices that do not include the rest of the roads that cannot be taken because of that first choice. The next turn eliminates more probabilities and so on.

Knowing all the probable paths of our life has a totally different meaning when one understands that we can exert our own choices within all the probabilities of our lives. I discuss this in even more detail below. What we view as the dark side of life, war, conflict, pain and hurt, whether physical or psychological, provides a means for spiritual growth. Whatever pain or pleasure we exert on others or even ourselves, we bring back to our higher self for self evaluation, not to be judged or punished, although negative experiences may appear to be punishment imposed on ourselves by way of our own judgment for something we might have done. Remember that there was no correlation between a life that was deemed to have done bad things and one that had done good things relative to a negative or positive NDE. This perceived dichotomy is being studied by IANDS, but no conclusions have yet been drawn.

We have chosen not only to come into this world to experience newness, but to work out a sort of contract we made with ourselves before coming. In the book *Irreducible Mind*, and the work of Ian Stevenson, *Twenty Cases Suggestive of Reincarnation*, there is compelling evidence that children with memories of past lives are in fact recounting real events. The fact that they returned indicates that their contract was not met. They either needed or wanted to experience more, or some interaction abruptly ended their sojourn, upon which they were promptly reincarnated to carry out their intended learning experience.

Roberta Grimes, in her book *Liberating Jesus*, has many interesting points about the words of Jesus Christ in the four Gospels of the Bible concerning reincarnation. Her arguments are viable and worth looking into. NDE'ers come back with information about their past lives. Psychologists are now successfully treating patients through past life hypnotic regression and even found that future life experiences can treat a patient's present problems using the techniques of hypnosis. Dr. Ian Stevenson made it his life's work, studying more than 2,000 cases of children that claimed they lived before and found veridical evidence of their stories.

An interesting point was made by researcher Leroy Kattein on NDE'ers that have attempted suicide. He says that we take our baggage with us to the other side. He talks about a young girl that attempted suicide by running a cardboard sled into a stone park bench. The light at the end of a tunnel met her. It told her she had to go back because it was not her time. She told the light that she didn't want to go back, that no one loved her. The light agreed and confirmed, "Yes, not even your mother. But your goal is to learn to love yourself." Where did this "goal" originate? According to many NDE'ers, we define these "goals" and then we live them out. Here is an additional point in support of a pre-life and reincarnation.

This young girl broke her neck, broke her jaw and smashed all her teeth. It took seven years of recovery before she could walk with crutches. She eventually became a counselor for young people who were suicidal. She was very good at it because she understood the reasons behind the motive to do this. Leroy goes on to say that the only difference between a suicidal action and not taking this action is a single thought. Suicide is not a viable option whether one succeeds or not. Firstly, if you don't succeed you may have to live the rest of your life with serious injuries that may impair your function. If you do succeed, you will leave a devastating impact on family and others that love you, and what's more, you may have to merely return and pick up where you left off.

This young girl did learn to love herself and to love others! What she also learned is that the Light has the power to send you back to carry out the contract you made with yourself.

Another NDE'er enforced the point that even if you don't commit suicide, if the lesson or lessons you made to yourself and the environment you placed yourself into do not produce the positive result intended, then you simply keep coming back until that contract is satisfied. I don't mean to sound like a broken record, but this is of importance. Physical existence is the most perfect environment of imperfection in order to impose any sort of spiritual growth for entities previously residing in a perfect realm. And it's not really a sure assumption on my part that the other side even is "perfect" by our definition of the word. As the physical universe is expanding, so is the spiritual realm by nature of the information being added to the grand library of All That Is. Like our belief that we are always right until a more clarified "right" comes into view, so too might the other side be perfect until a more perfect environment develops with added experiences.

If this concept of perfection is accepted, then our perceived state of imperfection is also perfect within the scheme of having an existence available in order to **grow** perfection. It's like what we call in engineering terms a closed loop system. This can be illustrated with the workings of a refrigerator. A substance is compressed, condensed, expanded, evaporated, and the cycle starts over. We are compressed into a physical form. The condensation can relate to our lives where we begin as vapor or spirit and condense to physical. This is the cold portion of our existence where we pick up physical content. After a certain amount of information transfer, or as in a real refrigerator, thermal transfer, we are pushed through an opening and expand back into an evaporated state of spirit where again, we transfer information to our higher selves.

What is transferred in an air conditioner is the temperature. What is transferred in the life cycle from non-physical to physical and back is the experience.

I don't know if this cycle goes on forever, but this may give illustration of the process of reincarnation and its purpose. This is simplistic and much more is going on within this basic illustration. The environment within the condensation phase, the physical, poses a complex hierarchical hypothetical as it does in the evaporative, or spiritual, phase.

According to people that have gone to the other side and come back to relate their experiences, we are all connected, we are all emissaries sent out into this physical universe to exercise the free will of choice. We are all tiny little gods, if you can accept that term without offense, sent out like drones with receptors so we can make sense of this physical environment and learn all sorts of things like love, life, about stuff, wonders of our world, the universe and each other. If we are in fact an extension of All That Is, God, the Source of all that exists, then wouldn't it be rational to think that this highest form of life possesses the same thirst, the same desire for expanding knowledge, the same type of life force as we do? Does the Source all-knowingly simply exist in static repose? I think not!

It's my hypothesis that God, All That Is, the Source of everything is dynamic and self-expanding. Sure, I believe that this intelligence is all-knowing, but knows all, up to the point of all that is, at whatever expanded state the physical and non-physical is at that point in its state of expansion. As that state expands, so does Its knowledge. And, since all time exists in the non-physical, I can only suggest that time is relevant only from the standpoint that actions govern the physical state of our universe, and all probabilities of those states exist in a non-physical thought-like environment. This reality is possibly where physicists have mathematically contrived multiple universes. In our physical universe, once that probability is chosen, its continuance collapses into the annals of historical memory we take back with us when we leave. More on this later as I postulate on Heisenberg's Uncertainty Principle, the collapse of the wave portion of light in its wave/particle duality as it relates to a non-physical consciousness of the mind.

The idea of a multiverse, a universe that breaks off into another physical universe and that one breaks off into yet another, makes no sense to me, as does the possibility that a ganglia of connected wires can have consciousness. Science and especially theoretical physics are replete with tricks of mathematics. These can mislead the logical mind into pigeonholes of illogic theories, and yet, reveal realities of the same that can and in fact do exist in the spiritual, non-physical, mental realm of what we laymen refer to as heaven. In such a heaven, anything that can be thought of is in fact possible, since it's a realm of existence that is comprised only of thought.

Can consciousness be implanted into physical objects as in the belief of panpsychism? Panpsychism is a totally out-of-date belief that, in their contorted ideologies, many researchers in the field of artificial intelligence indirectly or even directly support. Just as unrealistic as the idea that transferring my consciousness into a doorknob was, so is the concept that if enough wires or connections are tied to each other, voila, consciousness will appear. Artificial Intelligence (AI) is panpsychism. As much as programmers have tried to get computers to become self-aware, nothing more has ever come out of AI than that which was put into it. If anything comes close to having the number of electronic circuits required for self awareness, it's the global connectivity of the Internet. This would include every computer, every television, every cell phone, every modem and every GPS in the world. Not once has the Internet ever complained about anything, although it appears to, when bandwidth begins to choke communication. Yes, this includes Siri.

An example of the Internet's inability to "think" is illustrated by the updating of responses by Siri, the Ms. Know-it-all of cyberspace. On issues of rape and domestic violence, Siri generated responses such as, "I don't know what you mean," or "I don't get it." The authors of Siri, her creators at Apple, got in touch with all four companies that provide data for Siri's answers to improve these responses. It took the consciousness with the power of discernment of humans to add information to Siri's data base because she couldn't "think" of an answer.

Based on my research into life outside the body and my personal experience of having consciousness outside my body, I must conclude that the spirit of life doesn't fit within the realm of panpsychism. According to many scientists today, life predated the universe in a non-physical form and by design, our brains are the gateway that serves as the middle ground between our senses and the mind. It's a very simple concept to grasp. Since we can have awareness of mind without the brain, the brain, by itself, cannot be aware without the mind because mind came first, then mechanisms were created as a container for the mind in order to have a physical experience. I'm referring here to any and all living organisms, not just humans.

Thinking life exists in animals that have no central brain at all. Jellyfish have no central brain. They have one single opening to eat, reproduce and dispose of waste. One hole does it all! And, yet, without a central brain or what AI proponents have suggested as a minimum number of connections for life, these creatures have been very successful. Although they do have a form of nervous system, it's not the type proposed by AI engineers from which life can serendipitously spring forth. The jellyfish performs very complex behaviors, as does any other animal with a central brain.

Microbes are even more bizarre in their behaviors. Eshel Ben-Jacob was a pioneer in self-organization and pattern formations in open systems. In the 1980's he began studying bacterial self-organization. What he discovered was that bacteria have intelligence and complex social behaviors. He found that bacteria are smart cooperative organisms that employ advanced communication and lead intricate social lives within complex colonies. A bacteria colony will send scouts in search for nutrition for the rest of the colony. The colony will do all that's possible for self preservation; however, if a colony is split for a certain period of time, an alienation process occurs where, when the colonies are put in contact again, they will wage a war inhibiting each other from growing into a territory.

It was also discovered that bacteria exhibit preservation-making decisions. Without brains, they employ decision-circuits, if you can call them that, of individual bacteria that are coupled by an exchange of chemical messages that guarantee a collective decision for the preservation of the group.

The behavior and intelligence of bacteria to humans suggests that life, no matter how diminutive or gargantuan their "thinking" machinery is, must have some outside force for the animation process that motivates self preservation in the form of a creative process. What is also intelligent about bacterial life is that when confronted with chemical substances that threaten their existence, they will transmute and become resistant to that chemical. That's pretty smart. Remove even a single connection from an electronic system with thousands of circuits, throw just one drop of salty water on one of its integrated circuits, introduce an influence of magnetic pulse in its proximity and it will stop "working" and simply roll over and die. I know, this is my world and I've always said, "Electronics doesn't work, it just lucks out."

Artificial intelligence must therefore be considered as both a misnomer and an oxymoron.

The force that is life comes from a Source we have been shielded from for a purpose.

I believe that life is a perpetual force that's insatiably, relentlessly determined to delve into and learn from a myriad of new experiences. From years of searching, I've come to accept that the Source of everything, that Source we can comfortably refer to as All That Is or God is life itself in its purest non-physical **AND** physical form. I have also learned from studying near-death experiences that this Source has been distilled into one word—Love!

CHAPTER 16

AN ARGUMENT FOR GOD

Given all the evidence of near-death experiences, evidence of ghostly phenomenon, veridical events that cannot be explained other than that people can and do have consciousness outside their bodies, how can anyone still hang onto the belief that there is also no God?

ARGUMENTS FOR GOD'S EXISTENCE FALL CATEGORICALLY into ontological, causative, existence by design and the moral argument.

The ontological argument seeks to prove the existence of God by logic alone. It dates back to St. Anselm, an eleventh-century archbishop of Canterbury that argued once a mental grasp of the concept of God was fully understood, that God's non-existence was impossible.

The purported proof of the existence of God is the "first cause" argument also called the cosmological argument. This argument seeks to prove the existence of God merely by the fact that the universe exists. This argument states that nothing can come from nothing and therefore demonstrates the existence of a creator.

A third purported proof is argument of the universe from design. It's also called the teleological argument. The chance of the universe developing in such a way as to support life as we know it is so remote that it could only have come about by design. To be successful, this argument suggests the existence of a creator that takes an interest in humanity.

The fourth purported proof is the moral argument. It suggests that we only need to look at the authoritative nature of morality. The existence of moral laws demonstrates the existence of a being greater than us that rules over all creation.

Conversely, atheism is the position that there are no deities. There are two types of atheists. The weak atheist is simple skepticism, or disbelief in the existence of God, whereas the strong atheist holds the belief that God does not exist. Therefore, atheism is not necessarily a denial or disbelief of God, but rather a lack of belief, or a belief that there is no God. Atheists consider their disbelief in God intellectually fashionable. They argue that not believing that something is true is not equivalent to believing that it is false.

The agnostic believes that the question of whether a higher power exists is unresolved. In other words, the agnostic is someone who believes that we do not know for sure whether God exists.

George S. Greenstein, quoting F. Heeren in his book, *Show Me God*, page 233, said, "As we survey all the evidence, the thought insistently arises that some supernatural agency—or, rather agency —must be involved. Is it possible that suddenly, without intending to, we have stumbled upon scientific proof of the existence of a supreme being? Was it God who stepped in and so providentially crafted the cosmos for our benefit?"

Arguments for or against God have to be summed as philosophical. We can, however, make judgments on the existence of God based on evidence that we have at our disposal. The Bible says in Exodus 33:20 that no man has seen God and lived. In Ezekiel's vision of God and the chariot on which he was sitting appears to contradict this, as Ezekiel survived seeing God. The Bible also states in Revelation 10:7 that God is a mystery yet to be revealed. Throughout the Bible, God is referred to as somewhat of a combatant. In Exodus 34:14 he's referred to as a jealous God. Also in Exodus 23:27, God tells Moses that he will send his terror and will destroy all the people he encounters. And in Deuteronomy 3:6, God will fight for the nation of Israel and with God's help, they will kill all the men, women and children of every city. These words appear to be in contrast with the words of Jesus, who admonishes us to love our enemy.

The data coming back from near-death experiences paints a different picture from a militant stance that's more from the Old Testament, to a

God of love and understanding. In fact, few NDE'ers actually say that they were in the presence of God, but rather, that they *believed* or felt they were in his presence. Sylvia Browne mentions that most people "go through a tunnel and towards the light of God." Some say that they spoke with God. Thomas Sawyer says, "The light I am describing is whatever most people would describe as God. That's the description. It means the same as the word 'God.' It was in fact the light of Jesus Christ." Some say the Light *was* God. Reinee Pasarow wrote, "At this point I became aware that there was a light calling me from somewhere else, and I entered what people speak of as the tunnel." She goes on to say, "It was the love of God and the love of all things sacred and all things beautiful and all things just." The light never actually says that it is *the* All That Is, God, but there are implications that if the light isn't the ultimate Source, then, what or whom exactly is the light?

Who or what is God? Did we invent God or did God invent us? Did God create us? According to one definition of the light, it's the source of consciousness for everything in our reality. When in this presence, there seems to always be an overwhelming sense of love, comfort and warmth.

If God created the universe for our benefit and only for our benefit, of what benefit is it to God? Surely, there must be an underlying motive for its creation. There may very well be a reason for God himself to thrust out unimaginable energy to create a place just for infinitesimally small things to live. Compared to the size of the universe, we are extremely tiny, and yet in the quantum world, there are things that are infinitesimally smaller than us. I've entertained the thought that God may have created the universe for the fun of it! I also don't believe he created the universe for the benefit of little life forms—us, the animals, trees and bugs. And then again, thinking of God in the form of an entity rather than a force may be imposing into God something that God is nothing of the sort. I like the term Source, but don't always use it.

From the standpoint of logic, if the girl that attempted suicide was told that it was not her time because her lesson was to learn to love herself, doesn't it make sense that God also loves himself? In that light, just as God loves himself, we too should live in love of ourselves. As we love ourselves, life and the experience of life, wouldn't it make sense that All That Is, God, loves life, its experience and himself? Also, it's been said many times by NDE'ers that we are all connected, that everyone on the planet is connected. If the fact is that all life is connected and the light is the source of consciousness for everything in reality, then isn't God everything?

According to many NDE'ers, life is in and of itself All That Is fragmented into bits of self-contained entities able to experience certain physical aspects of the universe around them. All life has a purpose. That includes plant life and possibly even inorganic matter. I didn't say that inorganic matter can think, but has a purpose. I'll bring up an interesting discovery that I found in my research. A scientist believes that he has discovered that water has memory. This idea comes with a lot of controversy and the scientific community does not support the idea that was put forth by Dr. Jacques Benveniste back in 1988. However, a 2013 study from the Aerospace Institute of the University of Stuttgart in Germany supports the theory that water has a memory.

Some NDE'ers believe that the death of every form of life on this planet, or any other planet for that matter, recombines with its Source. All That Is adds to the experience of himself and through our experience of the home that is everything. In essence, life is God and God is life. And to push that envelope, if water has been found to have memory supporting the doctrine of panpsychism indicating that everything material has an element of individual consciousness, then the argument that God is everything is valid. I disagree, and rather say that God is everything, with the stipulation that the force of life is contained in everything that IS alive. We possess the God-like curiosity and never-ceasing life force moving ever forward into new and unexpected experiences to bring back to the Source, God, all that we've learned because we ARE GOD. Yes, that includes plants. The study that water may have some form of memory only supports the idea that something has been encoded rather than possessing the ability to think. This can be compared to the fact that a computer chip can be encoded with memory, but is not alive.

This brings me back to my shroom experience where, after my countdown, I shouted, "I'm God!" We are all God, connected in a matrix of consciousness of which we are also individualized for the purpose of expansion.

Scientists delve into the curious world of the unknown for various reasons. Many become researchers for benevolent reasons, to find new cures and feel good about themselves. Many get into it because government grants just don't run out—at least so far. And there are those that just want to know. They get on some quest to simply understand what makes things tick. Such was the case of an ex-CIA agent named Cleve Backster who hooked up a polygraph machine to a plant and recorded it "screaming" in pain.

Many people have duplicated his experiments and the general consensus is that plants do in fact feel pain. Not only to the degree that they are struck or uprooted, but they appear to have a psychic empathy toward other plants and even other life forms that are being hurt. Although this is an indirect offshoot of the subject of this book, the evidence of such a phenomenon can be seen on the *Mythbusters* YouTube video at: https://www.youtube.com/watch?v=fStmk7e9lJo

Today, many studies into plant behavior are being performed. It was discovered that trees help each other survive through what's called an internet of fungus. Suzanne Simard of the University of British Columbia in Vancouver says, "These plants are not really individuals in the sense that Darwin thought they were individuals competing for survival of the fittest. In fact they are interacting with each other, trying to help each other survive." My point for including this is not to prove that plants can think, talk or feel pain, or that they are conscious, but that life is interconnected in ways that baffle the imagination.

This supports the possibility that plants have a form of consciousness. If water has memory and plants have consciousness, are rocks and crystals encoded with some form of programmed data set? Did a glass doorknob somehow provide an opening for Shirley to connect with the non-physical and hence opened up a path through which Saiey could enter? Actually, I really despise this type of questioning without also providing answers. It reminds me of those undecided UFO videos that end with, "We are not being visited by extraterrestrials . . . Or are we?" C'mon, take a stand, either you believe in them or you don't! In this case, rocks being programmed or even thinking? I really doubt it. A glass doorknob opening up a channel? Maybe. Shirley channeling a spirit entity? Most likely. God being everything? That I believe! Whether this belief turns out to be absolutely true, I can only wait and see.

It seems like the more we learn about the universe, the stranger it gets. What many NDE'ers say about knowledge is that at a certain point in their experience, they come to a place that looks like a warehouse, a giant book or a huge room where anything and everything one ever wanted to know is stored. They say that when they are in this environment, they understand the meaning and purpose of everything possible, and that the answer to any question is instantly delivered. When they return to their bodies, this knowledge is completely left behind with the exception that they remember "knowing." I had a conversation with Beverly Brodsky, an NDE'er that has several YouTube videos, and what she said was, "I don't believe we're suppose to know." Again, memories are erased for a reason, and it only makes sense that that reason is for our spiritual growth.

The relatively new vocation of astrobiologist encompasses the search for habitable environments within and outside our solar system. One very interesting point an NDE'er mentioned was that she was taken on a journey of the universe, to distant galaxies and planetary systems. She saw many worlds with life, intelligent life on them. She said that the universe is literally teeming with life. She made another rather shocking comment, and that was that intelligent forms of life on other worlds don't know any more than we do about the afterlife! From this, we can draw the conclusion that supports the theory that Roberta Grimes put forth, that not only humans come here to experience spiritual growth by having their pre-birth knowledge erased, but this appears to be a universal aspect of life. And, by universal, I mean the entire universe. Someday I hope that contact with other beings is revealed to the public and the aliens come out and say, "Holy crap, you mean you guys have NDE's too?"

Given all the evidence of near-death experiences, evidence of ghostly phenomenon, veridical events that cannot be explained other than that people can and do have consciousness outside their bodies, how can anyone still hang onto the belief that there is also no God? I can only surmise that they have not looked beyond the end of their noses and simply wish to maintain their myopic views so that they can make themselves look good and be right. I dare say that it's much easier to disbelieve certain ideas than to be labeled some sort of a kook that believes in UFO's, dead people visiting God and watching plants talk to each other.

CHAPTER 17

THE MIND BRAIN PROBLEM

The mind, the set of cognitive faculties that enables consciousness, perception, thinking, judgment and memory has been caught wandering about outside the very heads they've been taught to reside within.

THE BOOK *IRREDUCIBLE MIND* LOOKS AT THE BRAIN AS A receiver/transmitter, or a gateway between the higher self and the "us" that we believe ourselves to be. It poses compelling arguments for the continuance of self after the brain ceases to function. The ever-growing number of cases of veridical perception supports this. Such cases include Pam Reynolds, who we discussed in some detail, describing a bone saw she had never seen before the operation and recollecting conversations during her brain tumor removal where she was clinically dead. A man named Ricardo, while during his resuscitation from a heart attack, saw a 1985 quarter lying on the right hand corner of a cardiac monitor and asked his doctor to verify this for him. His doctor found the quarter and documented this case. A woman with an obsessive-compulsive disorder about numbers remembered a twelve-digit serial number on a respirator while in a coma. These and many other cases are changing our perception of the brain's role in consciousness.

Albert Einstein brought space and time together as space-time. His reason for doing this is that space cannot exist without time and time without space. The two are interacting in a single mode. In order to have time, there needs to be a relative component from which to derive point A and point B and some linear motion between them. Time is irrelevant in the framework of nothingness as it relates to matter. Hence, in order for there to be physical space, there needs to be a component of linearity representing some travel of time between two points. The two are commingled and inseparable.

I believe that the mind and the brain are also in a state of "mind-brain" where the brain is the hardware used to interpret the physicality into which we are disposed. Our brains are connected to our senses that act like pickups or sensing modules of the physical body and the mind is akin to software, or program data we put into it. The more we sense of our world, the bigger the files, and the better our program can make sense of a situation. We can call it, "experience," having been around collecting wisdom. Our eyes are like photo-sensors relaying photon data to the occipital lobes of our biological computers. Our skin and other pressure sensors provide us with a tactile feedback from the spectrum of pain to pleasure. Our ears are the pickups that translate vibrating air into an electrical signal for the auditory centers of the brain to be interpreted into words, music or the pleasure derived from the sound of rain. We taste and smell with similar translations and interpretations. So begs the question, what—or better, who—is the interpreter of these signals? Is it the brain? Since we can have consciousness outside the brain, then it must therefore be the mind. Now the final question: Where is the mind?

In addition to interpreting, we can also ask where does the seat of emotion, the quest to learn, the desire to experience reside? Where is the "you" within, or possibly even outside the "you" that you believe yourself to be? Basically, the mind-brain problem is taking a new direction with the advent of veridical perception coming to the forefront. Researchers that have been collecting empirical data since Raymond Moody published *Life After Life* are postulating theories that fit the reality of veridical perception. Scientists that continue to hang onto the idea that the brain contains your entire consciousness and when it dies, "you will no longer be" will be considered as ridiculous as dues-paying members of the Flat Earth Society.

When the mind and the brain are considered as a single entity where the brain cannot exist without the mind, the concept of self becomes a bit clearer. The inverse of this is apparently not the case since the mind has been conclusively accepted by many near-death researchers as having consciousness without the brain. Therefore, the mind-brain differs a bit from space-time as space cannot be without time and time without space even though time is not fully understood. The mystery of time eludes us when gravity increases to the level of the Schwarzschild circle surrounding a black hole. This is the point of no return for any object going beyond this point, even the photon.

If physicists consider time as nonexistent inside the spherical envelope of the Schwarzschild circle, then is there a point at which the mind also ceases to exist? I think not. Therefore, rather than time being nonexistent, can we consider that beyond this point, time expands to infinity rather than collapsing into the infinity of zero? Isn't infinity both sides of the same coin comprising either nothing or everything? The feedback from near-death experiences has been that the realm of the spirit, or non-physical mind, is overwhelmingly, ineffably infinite. It simply cannot be described with the words that have an origin in physical reality where a beginning and an end parenthetically contain all that we can conceive. Could there be a correlation with the mind plane and the absence of time? Every person that has had a near-death experience reports that there was no time as we perceive it to be. Time was irrelevant and the past was as accessible as the future. Anita Moorjani expressed the past, as we understand it, as accessible. Conversely, she expressed the future in terms of probabilities, all probabilities. I found this term, probabilities, to be curiously in tune with physics.

Our sentient computers, our brains, are purposely limited in capability. If we were able to have the mental power to fully understand another person's thoughts or feelings, I'm sure there would be no conflicts between us. The fact that we have our own personal universe entrapping us within its boundary only serves to limit us to that which we believe. It's well known that our psyche also resides within the realm that it cannot be wrong until proven so, whereupon it merely modifies itself to a new right. However, if no proof exists, if no power of persuasion steps in to rectify a truly erroneous belief, then that belief remains in the "right" or "correct" category of our personal universe. Should another person's personal universe contradict that belief with a different one, the result is conflict, or even confrontation leading to violence. Because, in this case, two "rights" become two "wrongs," but only from the other's perspective.

I believe that this limitation is one that is at the foundation of the reason for our physical existence. The requirement for conflict is needed in order to experience and work out our plan for spiritual growth. Without it, we would in fact be living out the words of Rodney King when he said, "Can't we all just get along?" We can. We just need to be aware of the purpose for conflict and realize its necessity from a spiritual perspective rather than from the combative stance and the physics of conflict, which encompass many governing laws of the physical universe. The challenge with this idea is getting 7.4 billion people to be exposed to, understand, agree and then act on this principal. That's not just a tall order; I would say it's impossible. Although from the mathematics of probabilities, it's possible, but not for a long, long, long, etc., etc. time. I will therefore reiterate my first thought—it's impossible!

Can we surmise that the universe had therefore been created for the purpose of experiencing conflict? Could the Big Bang, a violent event of unimaginable proportion, have come about with the intent of producing rapid, faster than light expansion, heat to produce hydrogen and helium atoms? Then coalescing into stars so huge that when they exhausted their fuel, collapsed with so much pressure and heat as to produce heavy elements—iron, minerals and gold? Then, their dust from the outward explosion of material again began clumping together from gravitational attraction to form planets of all types and styles? And then, by some chance, little tiny life just happened? Was it all planned for the purpose of spiritual growth through experience of conflict? Or, did it just happen by chance?

The scientific method is defined as the best way yet discovered for winnowing the truth from lies and delusion. Its version is basically:

1. Observe some aspect of the universe.

2. Invent a tentative description, called a hypothesis, that is consistent with what you have observed.

3. Use the hypothesis to make predictions.

4. Test those predictions by experiments or further observations and modify the hypothesis in the light of your results.

5. Repeat steps 3 and 4 until there are no discrepancies between theory and experiment and/or observation.

And after repeating steps 3 and 4 until you are blue in the face, refer to:

6. God...

Many scientists that are now discussing the possibility of a God have had no religious affiliation. That's because they're simply stumped by the preponderance of data supporting that some prior energy had brought about the existence of the universe, and the lack of scientific answers as to how it could have come about by chance. The supporting facts of a Creator that they must concede to are:

1. The universe had a beginning.
2. The universe was balanced on the knife-edge that it ever came about at all.
3. DNA coding reveals intelligence.

Firstly, that the universe had a beginning, MIT scientist Dr. Gerald Schroeder is not the only scientist that has come to this conclusion. He explains that, for the first time, science has proof that the universe was created out of nothing. For something to come out of nothing there needs to be an acting force. His video, viewable at https://www.youtube.com/watch?v=eQVm8RokoBA, illustrates his reason for his change in the idea of God from non-believer to believer. He shows that before the physical universe, there was in fact nothing, as shown by the WMAP satellite. The diagram shows that the only law of nature at work is what's called quantum fluctuations that started with a set of forces that are not physical, acts on the physical, predated the universe and created physical particles from nothing. He then refers to this process as a definition of God. He goes further by saying that this force is still active.

In 1955, John Wheeler devised the concept of quantum foam as the foundation of the fabric of the universe. This is the boundary of astronomy and philosophy, since physicists cannot measure events shorter than Planck time, approximately 10^{-34} seconds. Before this, only imaginary, or Euclidian, time exists and therefore, the concept of nothingness is dirived.

Secondly, the chances of the universe ever coming about at all are, well, astronomical. Gestalt psychologists, especially Max Wertheimer, developed a number of "laws" that predict how perceptual grouping occurs under a variety of circumstances (Wertheimer, 1923/1938). Technically, in science, laws are predictions that are true. The law of symmetry posits that when the universe was created, there had to have been both matter and antimatter that annihilate each other. So, if they annihilate each other, then how did the universe come about? The answer that's proposed is that there was just a tiny bit more matter than antimatter, nearly perfect symmetry but not quite, and this tiny amount that was not annihilated is our universe. That must have been a really big bang!

A calculation that physicist Roger Penrose did on the odds of the universe coming about as it did are 1 part in 10 to the power of 10 to the power of 124. That's 1 followed by 10 to the 123rd power of zeros. As Penrose himself puts it, "that's a number which would be impossible to write, because even if you were able to put a zero on every particle in the universe, there would not even be enough particles to do the job."

Since I have a much, much better chance of winning the lottery, I'm stopping by the liquor store on my way home tonight. If I were a gambling angel at the time of the Big Bang, I think I would have thought twice on putting a bet on the universe ever coming into existence, let alone the complexity involved with the proliferation of life into it. We have been pondering the mystery of life since the beginning of intelligent thought on the planet. Today, scientists have been relegated to concede to the common denominator that some Big Guy in the sky must be responsible.

And, thirdly, as for intelligence in DNA, the Planetary Science Journal *Icarus* published an article that adds fuel to the growing stack of intelligent design articles. Dr. Vladimir I. ShCherbak, a mathematician at the al-Farabi Kazakh University of Kazakhstan and Maxim A. Makukov, an astrobiologist at Kazakhstan's Fesenkov Astrophysical Institute, wrote an article called, "The 'Wow! Signal' of terrestrial genetic code."

The abstract states:

"It has been repeatedly proposed to expand the scope for SETI, and one of the suggested alternatives to radio is the biological media. Genomic DNA is already used on Earth to store non-biological information. Though smaller in capacity, but stronger in noise immunity is the genetic code. The code is a flexible mapping between codons and amino acids, and this flexibility allows modifying the code artificially. But once fixed, the code might stay unchanged over cosmological timescales; in fact, it is the most durable construct known. Therefore it represents an exceptionally reliable storage for an intelligent signature, if that conforms to biological and thermodynamic requirements. As the actual scenario for the origin of terrestrial life is far from being settled, the proposal that it might have been seeded intentionally cannot be ruled out. A statistically strong intelligent-like 'signal' in the genetic code is then a testable consequence of such scenario."

The article goes on to say:

"But this criterion is equivalent to asking if it is possible at all to embed informational patterns into the code so that they could be unequivocally interpreted as an intelligent signature. The answer seems to be yes, and one way to do so is to make patterns virtual, not actual. That is exactly what's observed in the genetic code. Strict balances and decimal syntax appear only with the application of the 'activation key.'"

The questions remain: Was there energy prior to the universe coming into existence? If energy formed the physical universe, and life somehow sprung out of a hot big bang, what kind of force was it that produced matter and life? Furthermore, what is it within us, intelligent life, that drives us to think to ask where we came from? These questions boil down to an even more basic question: Doesn't it make sense that there was some form of energy able to perceive and experience subjectively that predates us? That's certainly oversimplified, but isn't that the question anyway? Where did we come from? How did we get here? And, what's our purpose? Those that have crossed the threshold and come back may actually have answered these questions. But for those that are skeptical of all that crosses their path, it's like not being able to see the woods through the trees. I've always said about staunch skeptics, "If a real UFO flew up their rear end, they still wouldn't believe in them."

I will start by reiterating that the most recent theories about the mind-brain dilemma expose that they are very separate and that the seat of consciousness is not contained within in the brain. The mind, the set of cognitive faculties that enables consciousness, perception, thinking, judgment and memory has been caught wandering about outside the very heads they've been taught to reside within. It's with great surprise that many people that have had a near-death experience look back at their body, many of which at first fail to recognize it as the vehicle they've just oozed out of. Dannion Brinkley, a very famous NDE'er, mentions that when he recognized the body lying there with purple stripes on its face as him, he said, "I thought I was much better looking than that." The purple stripes were the result of him being struck by lightning.

A Gallup poll was done in 1992 that found 5% of the adult population in the US had had a prior history of NDE's. This indicated that 13,000,000 people had a NDE in the US that year. This detailed study estimates that 774 NDE's occur in the US every day! Kenneth Ring at the University of Connecticut surveyed 102 people who had a NDE and found that almost 50% had had what is known as a "core experience" that included body separation. This could mean that 6,000,000 people, or somewhere around 350 people per day, experience consciousness outside their bodies.

With the proliferation of people willing the risk to be counted as insane, public exposure of accounts of NDE's are on the increase. When I first began my study of the phenomenon, there were only a few handfuls of YouTube videos and books on the subject. Today I peruse the net for new videos, purchase new books as they come out and strike this subject up with nearly everyone I come in contact with. That's when I discovered that one of my good clients had a NDE, a guy we used to ride motorcycles out in the desert with; even our gardener is in the fold.

Brian Miller was pronounced dead for forty-five minutes when his heart started beating again. During that time, he said he was very conscious, but in a different place. Psychological tests have revealed that memories of NDE'ers to be more vivid than any other memory. Belgian Dr. Steven Laurey, who studies NDE's, says that memories of these experiences bar all other memories hands-down for their vivid sense of reality. "The difference was so vast, even if the patient had the experience a long time ago, its memory was rich as though it was yesterday."

From these studies, it appears that memories of adult experiences in the near-death state that do not originate through the five senses and have not passed through the brain's filtering mechanism remain unblemished and fresh regardless of the amount of time that has passed. Every adult NDE'er telling their story has mentioned the same thing. Although this is not the case with very young children who lose these memories by the age of eight to ten years old.

During a life review, all memories, from the time of birth to the time the review was presented, were displayed in panoramic Technicolor, Dolby sound, with kinesthetic sensations and even the feelings of those they've pleased and pissed off are thrown in. It's as if the person were not simply experiencing their life, but reliving it with the added bonus, or possibly deleterious effect, of how they made other people feel, and even the cascading effect of third and fourth order of people that knew them. For example, someone that killed another person would not only feel the pain and suffering of the physical death of that person, but also feel all the sorrow and hurt of their wife, husband, children, relatives, coworkers and friends.

I theorize that all memories that are created or even uploaded into some non-physical data store remain unchanged, complete and in a perspective that far outperforms memories attained through our five physical senses. These types of memories are congruent with the evidence that they remain unchanging over time. This theory also supports the vivid recall we have with our life's review. I'm not alone supporting the belief that it's our consciousness outside the brain that's more fully connected with our 'greater self' mind. Or, in other words, a consciousness that is the mind residing outside the body. Many NDE researchers that support this can be found by looking up the IANDS website. This "outside the body" consciousness allows for experiencing multiple thought processes simultaneously and the cognizance that time during that state has little or no relevance.

In summation, the brain is merely an instrument of the body. It's the interpreter of the physical universe as picked up through our five senses, acting like a turnstile between our senses and the mind. Whereas the mind is the real us that resides in the environment of true consciousness, thought, which is the realm in which the spirit and infinity resides.

CHAPTER 18

PROBABILITY AND FREE WILL

If one can observe all time at once, then what is observed can only be every possibility, or better said, every probability of all future events. This vision can be a prelude to what one can live out, with the exception that with every turn that is taken therefore eliminates, or erases, the probable directions in which actions are not taken. This then allows for free will to play out its course in our physical lives.

I F YOU ARE NOT INTO PHYSICS, THIS CHAPTER MAY NOT MAKE much sense, as it deals with concepts of quantum laws that are difficult to perceive. I can only say that the quantum world is the closest we've come with science that pierces the veil of Newtonian realities into a new reality of strangeness that actually peers into the non-physical realms. It's a barrier, so to speak, that we've broken through with mathematics, but have only found scant evidence by way of experiment of the bizarre behavior of waves and particles on the edge between physical matter and the essence of energy and the collapse of time.

Kelly Sammy talks about her near-death experience in great detail. In it, she describes how she was able to understand that before we come into this world, we choose to be who we are, we choose the people we wish to be with, our children, parents, and friends. She also mentions that she doesn't know the mechanics involved, but that all that we experience in this life is seen before we are even born. As I've alluded to, this appears to suggest that we are predestined, or that everything that happens on this planet has been pre-scripted in some grand all-knowing of every future event. The reality of physics on the quantum level suggests that this is not as strange as it first appears.

Every near-death experiencer relates that time appears to have no meaning. They are in lockstep with their inability to describe just how time in that state appears to be more an aspect of mobility rather than an arrow into some future. The future and the past are as attainable or transcendable as any reality experienced in dreams. Kelly mentions that she doesn't like to even try to describe what a timeless state is like for fear that people will put tags of their rendition of their afterlife state.

What some physicists tell us about physical time is that it is an illusion. Physicists go so far as to say that our physical universe is nothing more than an illusion, that matter in the universe is mostly empty space comprising fields or forces. Mathematical equations pertaining to Newtonian Time fall apart in the quantum world. Two plus two make four for big stuff, but in the tiny quantum realm, as these minute particles and waves exhibit the limiting speed of the universe, time loses meaning and two plus two does not necessarily equal four. I'll try to simplify this as much as possible. For reasons known only in the quantum world, and mathematical equations of physics, two plus two, or more realistically, $X + X$ can equal all probable numbers. As time is relative to motion, which is the basis for calculating two points traveled within a space, in the quantum world, this calculation is not possible. It's called Heisenberg's Uncertainty Principle, where one can know an entity's velocity or its location, but not both. I, on the other hand, believe that when I stub my toe and it hurts, that was no illusion, that was real. Therefore, what's "real" to one person may only be their perception based on their ideas. Maybe for physicists, it's merely the product of intermingling physics with theory and philosophy.

Delving a bit further into theoretical physics, there's what's called the Reissner-Nordström Geometry that mathematically deduces that if one were to enter into a black hole, one would see what is described as a blue shift of light. Upon passing through the black hole and exiting it, you would be entering another universe where you would see a red shift. The significance of this ingress and egress of a black hole is that according to this math, all the information of the entire universe is contained in the infinite blue shift entering the black hole. Conversely, all the information of the future universe you have just entered would become apparent in its infinite red shift. If these mathematics are reliable, can it be possible that one residing in a non-physical mindset, where time location and speed has no meaning or reference are also able to see or experience their past, present and future in any location in the universe? This is precisely what people that have had a full-blown near-death experiences attempt to explain with little success of the reality of what they were able to effortlessly do.

This actually makes sense only if one understands that the strange laws of quantum physics don't follow the reasoning of how time, motion, gravity and distance are perceived in a three-dimensional space-time universe. In a timeless state, one does not actually see their future as much as the future is compressed backward into a finite state of all probabilities that one is able view. As difficult as this is to appreciate, it does not connote pre-destiny as much as it merely reveals all time compressed into an infinity of past, present, and future. What has not happened yet in our universe appears to be observable and changeable from that place in the timelessness of that infinity.

For example, we have all seen movies that use the past to change events that have happened in the future. This trick was used often in the film *Back to the Future*. The reality of seeing your life from that vantage point can be illustrated in events as written in that movie. In actually living out our probable script, whatever we choose by our own free will and volition rewrites the script by our choices and actions that we initially perceived in our non-physical infinity.

Anita Moorjani explained one particular event in an interview about her near-death experience when she stated that she could see her future in more than one linear possibility. She was told that she could return to her body, or she could make the decision to stay on the other side. In her own admittance, it was difficult for her to put all the events she experienced into sequence. However, she was able to clearly view not merely what led up to her getting cancer, but also see different outcomes of the decisions she could make at that moment. She clearly articulates experiencing all time happening at once and that whatever she thought of at that instant, so it was. Her book, *Dying to Be Me*, is highly recommended.

As in Heisenberg's Uncertainty Principle, one can know position or momentum (some use the term velocity), but not both. His formula predicts a probability, but not an exact number for both. This equation is perhaps the most famous next to E=mc².

$$\Delta x \Delta p > \frac{h}{2\pi}$$

Although the uncertainty principle applies to everything physical, it has little bearing or usefulness for large objects. In the quantum world, the very smallest of particles, where wave particle duality is exhibited is where this conundrum first raised its perplexing head. The uncertainty principle states that there is a built-in unpredictability in nature. This is exemplified by Schrödinger's paradoxical cat and box/dead or alive perspective that the cat is both dead and alive at the same time until such time as it's observed.

As difficult as it is for the layperson to understand, let alone accept such bizarre ideas, it is indeed a tenet of physics supported by verifiable and widely accepted mathematics. Quantum probability exposes a new and very different reality beyond the rules of Newtonian physics that once supported the notion that time and motion are fully predictable. These quantum laws of the microscopic world actually leak into the macroscopic world, but at an indiscernible level. If you accelerate you hand away from your body, the two have actually separated each other from their previous relation in time. Your hand is a little bit younger than your body because it has changed its velocity and mass properties by way of acceleration relative to your torso. That's why Einstein called it relativity.

A similarity exists relative to the uncertainty principle as it relates to the non-physical perspective view of probabilities. If one can observe all time at once, then what is observed can only be every possibility, or better said, every probability of all future events. To provide a comparison, Einstein concluded that if the speed of light is constant no matter how fast its source was moving, then the only thing left to modify was time. This was brilliant and radical thinking. Analogously analyzing the scenario of seeing all time, what is it that one **can** see if it has not actually happened in our space-time? If one experiences all time, the only conclusion that can be drawn is that one will see all probable future events rather than a single path that has not happened. This is precisely what NDE'ers attempt to explain. This is also what scientists have attempted to illustrate by suggesting a multiverse jutting out into all probable forms. Their mathematics has it right; they just missed the place where it happens. I believe it to be absurd that this occurs in a physical sense, but I accept the mechanism of being able to visualize probabilities in a non-physical environment.

This vision is a prelude to what one can live out, with the exception that with every turn that is taken therefore eliminates, or erases, the probable directions in which actions are not taken. This then allows for free will to play out its course in our physical lives. I'll try to simplify this. There's a wheel of fortune with one hundred numbers on it. You know that landing on any one number has a probability of one hundred percent. You can see the wheel landing on any number in your mind's eye before the wheel is spun. This game is slightly different in that you are in control of a lever that puts the brakes on the wheel. The physical reality of stopping the wheel from spinning with your lever and landing on a particular number has now eliminated all the other probabilities. In this case, all the other probabilities were collapsed by your choice.

Just for kicks and giggles, I will mention that there is a bizarre experiment of physics called "the quantum eraser" that affects the past of a particle by an action of changing its future. For more on this, I recommend looking it up on the Internet. This is real, folks! I won't get into this as I could write a complete book on this very interesting phenomenon.

An experience of all time at once, or that time has no relevance is difficult to imagine. Anita Moorjani provided a very good clue as to how it was possible to describe her existence where time did not exist. If everything was happening at once, then how could she describe her occurrence and then tell of that occurrence as having happened? It's because words, spoken one after the other are the only way she was able to do this in our linear time frames. However, in a non-physical realm of no time, it was possible to focus on a particular part of the volume of scenery that was available. Although she was aware of everything, it was the thought of focus that placed her in the area of interest.

Rich Kelly reveals a similar condition in his video of his near-death experience. He states that there is no space and time, that by focusing your mind on something, a tiny little spot, it becomes bigger. The notion of "moving" in that environment, he admits, is confusing. He poses the idea of what your life would be like if you weren't here. Admittedly, he encapsulates that that existence cannot be described in words, and says that the best way he can think of to describe it is, "you are."

To illustrate this timeless existence further, one can think of someone peering into a microscope and looking at a volume of microbes. All the microbes exist at the same time; however, it's the concentration of the focus on any one microbe that brings it into view. Let's assume that one can multiply one's self into an unlimited number of viewers, then an unlimited number of microbes can therefore be viewed and concentrated on simultaneously. This multiple self has the ability to fully comprehend, or focus on one microbe, several microbes or all microbes at once, at will.

A God-view of all creation can then be appreciated as an observer that knows all. In essence, all life and matter are emissaries broken out, dispersing like ever diminishing fractals into a physical universe and possessing the ability to ride out and experience any one of the probable outcomes of any entity that has free will.

And I'm going to end this chapter with a bit of humor. We've all heard about the God particle, the Higgs boson. Well, there's nothing special about the Higgs; in fact, it's just another elementary particle like the rest of the Standard Model comprising leptons, quarks and Gauge bosons. The Higgs boson was predicted in 1964 by six physicists, one of which was Peter Higgs. Physicists strongly dislike the term "the God particle" and call it sensationalistic. It was Leon Lederman, who was the director of the Tevatron of Fermilab in Batavia, Illinois, who spent years looking for it. If one is remotely interested in physics and entertainment combined, in his absolutely must-read book, *The God Particle,* about the invisible world of subatomic particles and the history of physics, it was Leon Lederman's humor that made it such a joy to read.

During his time as director of Fermi National Accelerator Laboratory from 1979 to 1989, he would toil each day in search of particles, one of which he was determined to find. As days, weeks, years drug on, one day he came into the lab, and told his staff that they were going to look for that "goddamn particle" again. Leon wanted to name the book *The Goddamn Particle* because of the high cost for something no one could find. So, in relating this event to his publisher prior to his book release, his publisher told him that they couldn't do that, but instead suggested that they name it *The God Particle*. And as Paul Harvey would say, "Now you know the rest of the story."

CHAPTER 19

WHY WE DIE

**"...living in one body forever is not as creative as reincarnation."
For us to reincarnate we require death.**

ACCORDING TO SOME NDE'ERS, YOU ARE NOT, IN THIS physical form, allowed the knowledge of creation, the wonders of the invisible realm of the spirit because if you knew, what would be the purpose of coming here? What would you learn? Nothing! You would already know the answers about the source of the universe and that would negate the purpose of physical life.

Think of the TV show *Naked and Afraid*. A man and a woman that don't know each other are put into a situation to live twenty-one days without food, water and clothes. They enter this trial with only an idea of what they are going to encounter. A few days into the experience, many begin to understand something more about what they've gotten themselves into. Somewhere farther into the journey, conflicts may arise, parasites in the water they drank may cause serious sickness, they may be nearly eaten alive by various bugs of a jungle.

Upon successful completion, most say that it was the hardest thing they have ever done and that it was the most fantastic and rewarding experiences of their lives. If they had known all of which they experienced ahead of time, would it have been that rewarding? Now imagine that they DID know everything, but only in all the probable outcomes. In other words, they would see themselves not making it twenty-one days. They

165

would see themselves die of thirst, or bitten by a poisonous snake, falling in love with their partner due to the cuddling to keep warm, and also making it through the ordeal—anything and everything that was probable. But in order for them to realize the agony of defeat or the thrill of victory of the experience, all knowledge of it was erased just before taking off all their clothes. In a similar way, we come into the world naked and afraid with no knowledge of what's in our future by way of choice. We live out the journey to learn and expand. Where, in the end of it all, as Saiey said, "This will lead you into such an enchanting experience that at the time of your physical death you can be reflected upon with the satisfaction that it was a job well done."

Coming into this existence of flesh from a realm of foreknowledge therefore cannot be of any learning benefit. From the standpoint of relating to each other, we would know that we are all part of the living source of All That Is. Fully knowing and understanding another person's "self," their points of view with all their experiences and knowledge that brought them into their belief system, would be like becoming them. If we could become them for an instant of understanding, all conflicts and differences would be quelled and it would be like saying, "I understand your point of view; however, my point of view is as what you have just fully understood."

What would be the point of full understanding? Not understanding is what gives physical existence its challenges and its beauty. It's so that we can learn new experiences on an individual basis and within our own personal life's quests. Therefore, the ability of 100% interpersonal understanding is not a provision of the grand plan. It's not like anything has been taken away from us, but rather put on hold for the duration of the physical experience. And, during that physical experience, we eliminate or collapse the paths not taken by way of the precious allowance of choice.

Within the physical timeframe of our life, we are continually uploading our experiences to our greater selves, a one-way communication channel that we recombine with upon our physical death. It's not always one-way communication, as sometimes we get help from our higher self or guardian, but for the most part, it is. Remember, upon recombining with our greater selves, we hence are shown our life in a full panoramic, stereophonic and better-than-Technicolor view, not only from our perspective, but from the perspective of everyone and everything we have interacted with while in the physical. This greater self, or possibly selves, accompanies us during physical life and also records and remembers everything we have done in detail that's only fully comprehended at the time of our life's review at our departure. It's true that not everyone has said they had a life's review with their NDE. That doesn't mean that reviewing the life you just left is not available. It only means that they didn't have one, or circumstances were different for them to have or not have one at that time.

Many individuals have recounted instances of a life's review without the typical NDE. Examples of World War II pilots may have temporarily recombined with their greater selves when they experienced a life's review just moments before they **believed** they were going to die as their planes dove toward their impending death. An incident was recorded of a man driving a VW Bug on a rainy night when a semi-truck came toward him on a head-on crash. In an instant he saw the back of his head from the vantage of a passenger sitting in the back seat, where he witnessed the entire crash and his full life's review at the same time. He then witnessed paramedics working on him. These cases are interesting because these people left their bodies before the accident occurred.

Our greater self may have more than merely a spiritual form. There was a case of a Canadian pilot that had a major engine malfunction in May of 2008 where his plane crashed through trees that ripped off its wings. He viewed the crash as if in slow motion and came to grips that this was the end. As he realized this, a peaceful calm came over him. He regained consciousness, hanging upside-down, bleeding from his injuries and fearing his plane would catch on fire. He exited the aircraft, taking paper towels with him to blot the blood off his body. As he sat down, he looked at the aircraft from the edge of a tree line, now about fifty feet away, and noticed that the captain's seat, his seat, was occupied. To his horror, he saw an arm and a leg dangling from it. He instantly realized that he was looking at himself. He then uttered the words, "F___, I'm dead."

At that instant, he lost consciousness. Four days later he woke up in the hospital with twenty-two broken bones, including serious head injuries. He met with the helicopter pilot that rescued him from the crash and told him of getting out of the plane, blotting blood from his injuries with paper towels. The helicopter pilot who rescued him said, "Captain, when I found you, you were hanging upside-down in your seat and you did not exit the aircraft." A further mystery in this case is that they found fifty-four blood-soaked paper towels in a trail leading to the edge of the tree line where he had viewed his body, which was still in the plane. Could this have been his higher self that took on a semi-physical form, experiencing the shared occurrence in some form of self-preservation? How could the trail of paper towels and the blood terminate at the location of the pilot's point of observation of himself dangling upside down from his seat that was still caught in the tree branches? See Jeff's fascinating video at: https://www.youtube.com/watch?v=YUNrBrHCT6s Or, typing, "Jeff's - NDE - Severe Plane Crash" in the YouTube search bar.

His experience also revealed to him that death was a "moment of peace and some understanding." "By seeing my lifeless body in the cockpit, I was suddenly aware of one universe and we're all one piece of the puzzle . . ."

In the near-death experience, many report this revelation of knowing or understanding a universal purpose where peace and love permeate throughout their surroundings. When returning to their physical bodies, this understanding and their knowledge appears to be taken away. Dr. Bruce Greyson, in his address to the United Nations on near-death studies, attributes the inability to convey these heavenly experiences to the limitations of language. In other words, we simply don't have words to describe the experiences on the other side. This is a fact of our language and explanations of these experiences may not incorporate the total answers. To this we must add that some NDE'ers themselves admit that knowledge that they were privy to was erased.

Contrary to adults having vivid memories of their NDE for the rest of their lives, very young children, those under five years old or younger, that have a near-death experience can recall their experience quite vividly for a few years afterward. As they reach the age of eight or ten, their memories tend to fade and they can recall less and less as time goes on.

Could this be part of the grand plan for physical experience for the very young, not to remember anything about a non-physical existence we will all someday regain? To experience the newness of a life as if one had never existed before can only come by having the previous one erased. I'm not implying that we all reincarnate from past lives specifically, but from the many incidents of those who have had a near-death experience, many report of a previous existence. Others may come to experience the physical from a non-physical existence for the first time.

To explain our human behavior from this viewpoint, it is of prime consideration just what we can do in the physical that we cannot do in the non-physical and vice versa. What have we learned from near-death experiencers about existence on the other side? What is it that differentiates heaven, or what we can label as heaven, from this earthly plane? We know that on the other side, there can be no misunderstanding of what it is that another non-physical entity is conveying in their communication. The receiver of this type of telepathic transfer knows precisely what the sender is intending to "say." And there is no doubt about its clarity. Words are not used; therefore, their definition does not stand in the way of any sort of miscommunication. Take the word "love." People often start to define love with, "Well, to me love is. . . ." And with all the words that we use on a daily basis having slightly different to radically different meanings for different people, it's no wonder that we don't convey exactly the same intended message. This is made even worse trying to communicate with someone whose native language is other than yours. I love Rosaline in French Canadian and she loves me in Chinese? Maybe . . .

To add insult to injury, here in the physical we can do much more than simply miscommunicate. We can lie. If there is no misunderstanding on the other side, we have a **gift** in the physical that not even the Angels of heaven can exercise. I use the word "gift" for emphasis. I debated whether to call it a capability, a capacity or potential. The term "gift" seemed appropriate in what many deem as an *imperfect* world. Interestingly, in the Bible they call the Devil "the father of the lie." This is when he told Eve that they would most certainly not die if they ate of the tree of life, or what some refer to as the tree of knowledge of good and evil. If you believe in talking snakes, he had to have done this in a physical form, or lower vibrational realm, or else he would have been busted right then and there. So, lying is one advantage (if you want to call it that) that we have, that higher non-physical entities don't have.

There is a dichotomy in the data I've gathered as to whether one can lie in the lower realms. One example comes from a description from Howard Storm, an NDE'er that mentioned that entities he was in contact with in a lower, hell-like environment were "lying" to him. After he was raised from that environment, a pure environment of love surrounded him. Howard has several YouTube videos of his experience and how it's changed his life.

The next "gift" is one that should be very obvious. There are no actual things on the other side. Everything is comprised of thought. One near-death experiencer describes in her video how she changed her scenery by thought. She had read about near-death experiences, that one can imagine being somewhere, and in an instant, there they would be. So, she decided to imagine herself in a beautiful, lush pasture and immediately there she found herself. Remember Dr. George Ritchie who wanted to go to Richmond, Virginia after "dying" in a military hospital? He found himself flying extremely fast just above the ground and he eventually was where he wanted to be. Having the ability to manifest your place or surroundings by thought alone redefines the reality of perceived objects. It also allows for mobility by the process of thought.

Objects are the products of physicality. Mental manifestations connote an evanescent ownership only while the thought is alive and present. Those thoughts, although they are your own within your existence as a non-physical entity, no other entity, whether in the physical or non-physical, can take it away. We, on the other hand, are here in the physical. Being surrounded by physical objects, we therefore possess the gift of thievery. Essentially, you can't steal thoughts but you can steal stuff. Therefore, if one's surroundings are manifested by thoughts, it's impossible to steal them over there. Compulsive thieves may die, but what are they going to steal, your thoughts? And, furthermore, why steal anything when all one has to do is think of it, and poof, there it is! Stealing is a convenience of the physical. In other words, there are no thieves in heaven—what a deal!

Deceit and cheating are also worldly gifts. If one cannot be untruthful, they're thought of as compulsive liars. Deceit is also a thing we can do here that we won't be able to do in the higher planes. The games people play will be over. You won't need to rehearse to be yourself. It's the land of the WYSIWYG, What You See Is What You Get. Pretentiousness or faking it can't follow you into the higher planes of afterlife. We all have, at one time or another, put on airs, either to impress others or maybe even ourselves. That will be over with. To go a step further, we may exaggerate or even lie in order to trick or mislead. There? It ain't gonna happen!

Fighting is a gift we can experience while here on terra firma. Think of the octagon that the UFC fighters get into to beat each other's brains out. Why do they do it? For me, it's obvious why. Think about it for a few minutes. Just like in a Hollywood movie, punching a ghost just doesn't work. Here, we can exercise our physical prowess, our machoism. We can also prove how right we are and how wrong someone with opposing views is by simply knocking them out. Getting rid of the opponent makes the problem go away. Where am I going with all this? The obvious may be raising its head.

Firstly, I should say that we must remain pragmatic about theories, yes, even me, when I believe I have found some answers to where Mom and Dad are. Today I know much more than I did several years ago. I continually search for new knowledge and add reports of people that have been to the other side to my repertoire.

I now have a new appreciation for God while actually having my ideas of religion as a whole deflated. Although religion has had its share of responsibility for some of the most gruesome mass killings, right up there with political ideologies, good people of faith will cling to the positive aspirations written down in their principles.

Mellen-Thomas Benedict put it bluntly in his depiction of his NDE's. When he asked God what was the best religion on the planet, what he refers to as Godhead answered with great love, "I don't care." Mellen-Thomas Benedict goes on to explain that he went over to the other side with other concerns and fears, such as toxic waste and nuclear weapons, and came back loving every problem we've created for ourselves. He says, "I love the mushroom cloud; this is the holiest mandala that we have manifested to date, as an archetype." Where was he going with those statements?

Just like the day I broke Huck Graham's arm and he showed up on my doorstep with his outstretched inverted left hand, war and fighting have had a yin-yang effect on societies past and present. Just as Japan aggressively bombed Pearl Harbor, we in turn defeated them with the destruction of Hiroshima and Nagasaki by dropping atomic bombs on them, and then made a treaty to protect them against aggression from communism by signing the Treaty of Mutual Cooperation and Security.

Ironically, it was Genghis Khan, who slaughtered millions in his conquest of most of Europe, Central Asia and China, that instilled meritocracy over dictatorial leadership and encouraged religious tolerance.

Why do we lie, cheat, steal and pretend not to be ourselves? And most important of all, why do we fight?

To make these a bit more palatable, I will offer my theory after the following series of questions. Why do our leaders commit to forms of aggression and put millions of people in the path of death itself? Why do those that want to kill us actually take action and attack us? Could it be that we fight because we don't know what the other side is thinking? Do we fight because we believe in some outdated or worldly doctrine, political or religious? Or could it be for the "stuff," territory? Do we fight over differences in philosophies of governing the masses—or because our neighbor's dog won't stop barking? Or could it be a much simpler underlying motive? We can't fight or kill each other on the other side because we are already dead, at least in physical form. Do we do it here for the mere experience, or as suggested, our spiritual growth just to see if we *can* love our enemy? Or, is there a multitude of reasons for what we perceive are **all** the negative aspects of life here in the physical?

My take is that it's a complex issue, and not only a combination of all the above, but reasons that may not be clear to us because of the limited nature of the linear thinking capabilities of our brains. Some day we will all have our consciousness fully uploaded, or transferred to our higher self's mind in a non-physical existence where thought allows an expanded, unlimited spherical understanding of things we, as some NDE'ers say, "are not allowed to know." This will include not only the present life we've just experienced, but possibly many past lives, and also a merging with universal knowledge on higher planes. Until that time, we must live out the experiences and consequences we chose for ourselves.

Why do we die?

Mellen-Thomas Benedict says, "Earth is in the process of domesticating itself." As for our bodies, he states that through scientific discovery, we may unlock the secrets of living forever, but adds that living in one body forever is not as creative as reincarnation." For us to reincarnate we require death. The key word that caught my attention here was "creative." Even death appears to be some form of creative process, or a re-creative process in order to expand and learn from the aspect of the new. Being born from organic matter and somehow having the force of life projected into it must have a purpose if one believes in a creator. I don't believe we come into existence to learn things like mathematics, how to make electricity, build giant cruise ships, study the biology of cells down to the genome, for the purpose of having it taken away due to the dying of a perfectly good brain.

On the other hand, all of our activities seem to revolve around human interaction and the results thereof. We don't take anything to the other side except our thoughts, and if our thoughts focus more on physical things, well, we're out of luck as to the purpose for bringing these back, aren't we? If we die in order to bring with us the experience of having cared and loved, and along with it the beauty of experiences of this physical universe with others, then wouldn't this be the treasure trove representing what we've accomplished with our lives?

CHAPTER 20

MOM AND DAD—I FOUND THEM

What I do truly believe is that they are somewhere! And that they aren't nowhere.

IT'S MY DESIRE THAT MY SEARCH FOR MY MOM AND DAD HAS enlightened anyone that's lost a loved one. It's very painful to think that you might never see them again. I know it was for me. For many years I was very bothered at looking at my mom's photographs. It brought back the hurt and unfairness of this life, that anyone could be ripped from you by the clutches of death. My heart still sinks when I see my mom and dad's pictures. With the exception of memory, I can only see their form entrapped within the little grains of pigment that's all of what's left of them in the photographs of this world. Thought is what brings a bit of their lives into my soul as I mentally listen to my dad playing his guitar with Mom harmonizing songs in the little living room they had built from scratch.

I can see my dad on a Saturday morning, still half in the bag, standing in front of our living room's large picture window wearing nothing but his underwear, praising the Good Old Lord for the beautiful trees across the street. I remember my mom bent over in the kitchen when something went wrong with the washing machine, "Goddamn, son-of-a-bitch," she blurted! I was appalled at my mom's potty-mouthed expletive. No, she wasn't foul-mouthed, that's why I was taken back. She was human! She was real! And she was loved!

George Washington and my mom had something in common. Neither ever told a lie. Although I'm not 100% sure about George. My dad, on the other hand, was an exaggerator extraordinaire. When he caught a fish that weighed five pounds, it was always a ten-pounder. Then, he would turn to my mom and say, "Isn't that true Colombe?" where my mom would nod her head, then when no one was around, she would say, "Why do you put me on the spot like that, can't you just tell the truth?" And here I say again, he was human! He was real! And he was loved!

No matter how righteous, how moral or virtuous one believes himself or herself to be, or how well these attributes are exalted upon someone else, there will always be a fly in the ointment, a crack in the foundation. Even Mother Teresa herself had doubts about the existence of God. She was doing work in Calcutta when she began to doubt. In one of her letters to a friend she wrote, "Where is my faith?" She went on to say, "Even deep down there is nothing but emptiness and darkness. If there be God, please forgive me." In a different letter she questioned, "What do I labor for? If there be no God, there can be no soul. If there be no soul then, Jesus, You also are not true."

After her death, Mother Teresa came under fire for taking in millions of dollars and running a less-than-adequate facility. Some have questioned where all that money went. She adhered to the Catholic doctrine and was quoted as saying, "There is something beautiful in seeing the poor accept their lot, to suffer it like Christ's Passion. The world gains much from their suffering." In any organization or activity there will always be supporters and those that disagree. No matter what we do, we are here and they are there. Only Mother Teresa can judge her actions according to her spiritual expectations, and those of us remaining can sit on the sidelines judging from a worldly perspective. We judge from our infinitesimal and limited perspective, and God observes with no judgment, but only love. It reminds me of the Pink Floyd lyrics in the song *Us and Them*. We demonize our own kind by voicing our displeasure about another's activities, beliefs and opinions. On the higher planes, there is no "us and them," but a desire for sharing experiences in a voluminous state of love. On lower and mid-planes, there appears to be some coarseness relative to one's thought-state, but ascension to higher orders appears to be goals that are worked for.

When we die and ascend to higher planes, all the separation, being to being, soul to soul becomes moot, ineffectual. The only thing that matters on the other side is what we had done with our lives when we were here in the physical, not what others had done to us. The perspective of our life is viewed from our own vantage point, not from any others, including God's. This is borne out of NDE'ers reports of their own self judgments of their lives.

Mom and Dad had their life's review and judged their lives according to their own standards. It appears that we will all do this. They may have moved into that realm of thought, making an environment for themselves in some of the strata that allows for it, or they may have moved upward into a higher vibrational plane where learning is of greater motivation. I don't know how to get in contact with them. By the fact that it was his guns that fell over without anyone touching them, I believe it might have been my dad that found some hole between his possession, the guns and wherever he was to let me know he was around. I am also of the belief that it might have been him that was able to make the piece of foam core beat between the wall and a bookcase. Changing a margarita's taste to his favorite mixed drink and appearing with that unmistakable plaid shirt are events that I have to keep reminding myself of as actually happening. As strange as these occurrence were, I can't think of any other reason for these things to have happened.

Self-judgment doesn't mean that truly evil people judge themselves from a standard of evilness. The lower vibrational levels provide a wake-up slap in the face for evil thoughts. Ascension with evilness of thought is not possible. If one actually likes it there, then that's probably where you belong. I have yet to read about anyone that thought this was a place they were comfortable with. That doesn't mean that a truly evil person wouldn't want to remain there.

Contacting dead loved ones has stirred much curiosity and belief in that certain people have that gift. John Edward, James Van Praagh, Theresa Caputo and others have gathered a large following of believers.

I'm impressed with a young Hollywood medium named Tyler Henry that's gained much notoriety with his television show. I have to admit that contacting the dead through a medium has a very different format than people that have had a NDE. While lots of information about the afterlife comes from NDE'ers, not much about the conditions over there comes from mediums or the people they've channeled. Although names, dates and events are deemed accurate, the messages replicated over and over is that they are okay, that they are aware of the ones they left behind and that they don't want them to worry.

Maybe next, I'll do some extensive research on how to contact those that have crossed over. There are many techniques on the subject and much to research from.

I named this chapter, "Mom And Dad, I Found Them," but quite frankly, I haven't actually found them. What's important to me is that I truly **believe** that they **are somewhere**! And that they **aren't nowhere**. This belief by itself is a consolation that any bereavement that I may have had in the past about them can be replaced with the joyous knowledge that I've gained by looking for them. I've discovered that the evidence points toward a continuum of life that is rich with experience. I've learned that Mom and Dad are themselves, and that they brought with them all the memories of their life and the love they had for each other and their "boys."

I've learned that they may actually return and have a new experience with physical life, or they may choose to ascend through layers of increasing spiritual growth.

I'm comforted by the knowledge that they fit the profile of regular people that were humble, believed in God and a heaven that was going to welcome them, take them in and provide guidance in their transition.

For this I thank all the brave people that have come forward to tell, in the best way they could, about what they experienced during their NDE. Each story, each definition of the afterlife, each description, no matter how intricate or simple it might have been, has added to the growing compendium that's slowly merging into a New Bible of knowledge about heaven, God and what we are all going to someday experience. This work also provides a new baseline for living our lives with an expanded understanding of love.

EPILOGUE

EXISTENCE IN A NON-PHYSICAL REALM HAS BOTH ADVANtages and limitations. Advantages in the non-physical compared to limitations in a physical body include the ability to think yourself to any place in the universe, and there you can instantly be. They include reading and sharing thoughts of other entities, both physical and non-physical. Having vision that allows one to see through physical objects. The merging with other non-physical entities in order to share that being's total experience and all the knowledge that that being possesses. In that state, one can imagine surroundings and they appear in a reality more real than our own physical experience. It's a complete immersion into that created environment with every detail, color, smell, texture, auditory sensation and even flavor of your creation. There is unimaginable mobility, even in multiple directions and consciousness at once. However, there are limitations too. In the higher realms, one simply cannot lie, steal, cheat or deceive. Striking out as if to harm someone physically, of course, is also not possible. One cannot hide, for there is nowhere you cannot be found. You also cannot die! Any desire to exercise these limitations will automatically eject you from the higher realms—in essence you've been demoted.

Before we are born, we have a desire to experience physicality. In other words, we come into this physical world knowing full well what types of experiences physical existence can offer, but not actually have experienced it. On the back end, people that cross over to the other side are sometimes not aware of their physical death until they are met by deceased relatives, or perhaps some entity that has been watching over them, like a guardian angel. They eventually realize what has happened to them and most will go with the flow, so to speak. Non-physical entities that have never been physical, wanting to experience physical existence, are able to merge with them to get a "download" of that person's experiences when they were alive on Earth. This can trigger a desire to experience physicality for themselves.

Along with the desire to experience a physical existence, a plan of what type of experiences we/they wish to have is laid out. Call it a contract with ourselves that we create in order to fulfill some desired end result or to come here merely for the experience. As many people as there are on the planet, so too are the diversified desires and reasons as to what sort of experience might unfold as a result of that contract. One might wish to experience the thrill of winning through competition. Another might wish to invent and create things out of the materials of this world. Another might have the desire to experience power over others, or the satisfaction of control. Still others may wish to engage in loving acts of giving. What we innately are may stem from that contract with ourselves before we ever came into this existence.

Debates have raged on for decades as to whether it is nature or nurture dictating who we are or who we become from birth. Scientists have mostly come together and are of the opinion that it's a combination of both genetics (nature) and environment (nurture) that comprises our personality, and hence, behaviors. However, there are certain unanswered reasons for behaviors that don't come from either side of these mechanisms. For instance, why do some babies come into this world with full-blown personalities from the moment they arrive, or even inside the womb they appear to respond differently to certain stimuli? This certainly cannot be environment. However, it can be attributed to genetics. There is a problem with that scenario also, and it falls within the scope of the fallacy of the single cause. This is when it is assumed that there is a single cause for a given event.

Oversimplification is a common fallback in deducing reasons for situations that may have complex causes. For example, a mother might say, "My son was caught stealing the car because he was hanging around with the wrong crowd." Really? I'll bet the mothers of every single member of that "crowd" said the same thing about her own beloved child. "The serial killer was a victim of his environment." But what about the environment? Did it also include an abusive teacher, an influence of mind-altering substances (I should talk . . .), a movie that glorified a band of bank robbers as some sort of heroes, a few too many tickets given to him by police doling out terse advice? Or, could it have been a contract with himself before he ever came into the world?

The idea that we existed prior to our birth in an environment devoid of physical experiences poses a tantalizing theory. Never having a physical experience may very well provide the impetus to try it out. From the good to the bad, being in a physical form may stimulate one to have a totally new and exciting experience to bring back into a non-physical existence. And then, if further growth is desired, we do it again under a different set of circumstances. The diverse number of possibilities available on our planet is very enticing. What does it feel like to win the Grand Prix or be the first man to make it to the top of a certain mountain? What was it like when Neil Armstrong stepped off that ladder? I often think, "Boy, if I were young again, I'd love to experience doing a back flip on that bike."

On the other hand, there are thrills that certain members of our human family engage in that are horrible. Charles Manson has the notoriety of being the most evil man alive. I can't imagine what sort of contract he made with himself.

It's my understanding that the majority of us would never wish to engage in these sorts of behaviors, as there are vibrational consequences on the other side. However, the question in my mind remains, why do people engage in abhorrent acts? And why do victims of their crimes maintain no animosity toward these souls after arriving on the other side?

When on the other side, any scenery, every scenario, invented with the intent of negativity will reduce your vibrational status. Doing this will automatically plunge you into one of the lower levels where a good description of that environment is described in the Bible as, ". . . there will be weeping and gnashing of teeth."

In all my research, I've found no evidence of a perpetually burning hell, but lower levels of the spirit realm indicate that there is a place where despicable things occur and atrocious scenery can be experienced. So, in a sense, it is possible to create a negative environment for yourself in the afterlife, but you can't do this without consequences.

Our choice to experience this world can temporarily separate us from God, but never God from us. Death unites us with our greater selves. By the time we leave this world, we fully know who we are by the judgment we impose on ourselves. We also know that we are loved by that Source from which we came because we are all connected. We discover that we are all one with and from God.

Living in the present physical state is a gift we give to ourselves out of choice. We choose to come here. We choose what we want to learn. In that process of working out our contract we delineated, we can be assured that whatever it was that we chose, it was for a purpose. That purpose may include our spiritual growth, to gain something from the physical experience and to bring the entire experience back to that Source that is continually expanding. And, for the plan of the universe, God is not finished!

Ivanhoe Chaput

www.ingramcontent.com/pod-product-compliance
Lightning Source LLC
Chambersburg PA
CBHW061509050726
47593CB00002B/508